# Canadian Converts
## The Path to Rome

### Essays by

**Conrad Black**
**Kathy Clark**
**Douglas Farrow**
**Ian Hunter**
**Amy Lau**
**Richard John Neuhaus**
**Eric Nicolai**
**Jonathan Robinson**
**Jasbir Singh**
**Lars Troide**
**David Warren**

**Justin Press**

Canadian Converts
The path to Rome

is published by

Justin Press
730 Parkdale Avenue
Ottawa, ON K1Y 1J6

613-729-2247
www.justinpress.ca
jdlg@rogers.com

Legal Deposit, 2009
Library and Archives Canada

ISBN 978-0-9813184-3-1

Cover image: Toward Calvary
a painting by Michael O'Brien
www.studiobrien.com

# CONTENTS

# INTRODUCTION

Perhaps the most frequently quoted line of the late Pope Paul VI is that "modern man listens more willingly to witnesses than to teachers, and if he does listen to teachers, it is because they are witnesses."[1] Certainly those of us who work with young adults know that the personal testimony has become an almost essential element of Christian youth gatherings. Our culture wants to hear testimonies of truths lived concretely rather than truths explained abstractly. We search for witnesses, not teachers.

The witness of converts holds a certain fascination in the Catholic mind. How does a person make the decision to change one's path, reorient one's thinking, convert one's heart? Cradle Catholics like me often find the stories of converts fascinating precisely because they are so alien to our own experience. The indifferent, lapsed, sinful, and even self-loathing Catholic often testifies that once-a-Catholic-always-a-Catholic. Might the testimony of converts explain why that is so? Of course, we also find in convert stories a source of pride, namely that others would wish to become what we are. There is encouragement too, that despite all the manifest troubles here and there in the Catholic Church, she still attracts those seeking Jesus Christ.

It would be better to say that converts have had a particular experience of the Lord Jesus seeking them. Those of us raised as Catholics grow into, one hopes,

---

[1] Paul VI, *Evangelii Nuntiandi*, 8 December 1975, #41.

a sense of being chosen before we were even capable of choosing. The adult convert to Catholicism experiences being chosen by Christ in a direct and vivid way. That choosing often confirms and brings to fulfillment an earlier being chosen through a valid Christian baptism outside the Catholic Church.

Each conversion story tells the tale of how one has been chosen. The writers in this collection focus, as one must, on their response, but before there is a response there needs be an invitation. Conversion stories are evidence that the Lord is still inviting souls to follow Him into the fullness of truth in the Catholic Church.

Cardinal Joseph Ratzinger once noted that there are as many paths to God as there are souls. This collection indicates something of the variety of those paths, even if the preponderance of these stories emphasizes the intellectual journey toward Catholic truth. There are a number of intellectuals in this book, but even for some who have devoted themselves to the intellectual life, like Father Jonathan Robinson, it was a mysterious experience of God's presence that led to the final decision to convert. It brings to mind the late Avery Cardinal Dulles, SJ, perhaps one of the clearest theological minds of his generation. He decided to become Catholic as a young man at Harvard not so much because of arguments but because of the wonder and beauty and order he beheld in a tree blossoming in the springtime. There are many paths indeed.

For Father Eric Nicolai it was the sincere friendship of a devout Catholic that set him on his way from Lutheranism to the Catholic Church and eventually the priesthood. For Kathy, it was her future husband who prompted her to discover that the Jesus of Nazareth she read about in the Gospels was indeed the fulfillment of the Jewish faith into which she had been born. Amy Lau too became Catholic with her husband, who first prompted her to consider Christianity when he himself was not a Christian. For Jasbir Singh, it was potential tragedy that provoked a consideration of life's meaning. The initial fruit of that consideration was a descent into dissolute living, before he escaped that emptiness through an encounter with the Lord's mercy. Two of our contributors were influenced not by those close to them but by Pope John Paul II, whose clear witness was compelling to them in a religious world marked often more by confusion than clarity. Ian Hunter entered the Church at the end of distinguished university career, Douglas Farrow closer to the beginning. The latter's account, this collection's longest, calculates with exact precision the degree of assent he was capable of giving to the truths of the faith when he converted. For Conrad Black, it was a willingness to acknowledge that, on balance, the Catholic faith offered the most plausible account available to explain his more general conviction that God existed and that a spiritual principle is at work in the world.

I have never doubted the truths taught by the Catholic Church. John Henry Cardinal Newman, the greatest of the English-language intellectual converts, is often quoted on his view that a thousand difficulties do not add up to one doubt. But I have not had a dozen difficulties, let alone a thousand. Perhaps it indicates a less adventurous cast of mind.

Yet I consider it the grace of my life that I have been a happy, confident Catholic my whole life. I have never even thought about being anything other than a practising Catholic; I cannot even imagine seriously considering the question.

Thus I have deep admiration for those who have had to wrestle with such questions that go to the depths of one's identity. Frequently the decision to convert ruptures the other sources of identity – family, relations with friends, participation in one's own culture and nation. My identity, formed by my parents, both daily communicants, is simply Catholic. Yet over time, those who have converted to the faith have greatly shaped the Catholic and the priest that I have become.

In 2010, John Henry Cardinal Newman, patron of the Queen's university chaplaincy where I serve as chaplain, will be beatified. For many years, I have regarded him as the model of the Catholic intellectual life, and his sermons have provided spiritual nourishment and homiletic inspiration since my seminary days. I also think him the greatest prose stylist in the English language, an opinion I share with Lord Black of Crossharbour, who has a contribution to this volume, itself illustrating the effect of Newman on his own conversion. (Lord Black would include Abraham Lincoln alongside Newman as a master stylist and I would have little objection.)

I have learned more about sacred scripture from the twentieth century's most sublime English-speaking preacher, Monsignor Ronald Knox, the convert son of an Anglican bishop, than from my university scripture courses. His books of sermons and spiritual conferences remain the most frequently consulted on my bookshelves.

My formation for the priesthood began at St. Philip's Seminary in Toronto. The Fathers of the Oratory of St. Philip Neri run the seminary, the rector of which is Father Jonathan Robinson, another contributor to this volume. Father Robinson was somewhat distant from us students during my time there, but the animating spirit of the seminary was and remains Father Paul Pearson, another convert, who gave a definitive shape to my priesthood and my thinking approach at the beginning of my formation.

One of my principal intellectual influences was the late Father Richard John Neuhaus, whose theological and personal essay on his own conversion is reprinted here. It's worth the price of the book alone. He later became a valued mentor and dear friend. He preached at my first Mass, and provided wise counsel and encouragement along the way. When he died in January 2009 it was my great honour to preach his funeral Mass. Some of my best friends, as they say, are converts to the faith. Those in the public life, like Jason Kenney, Canada's most outstanding Catholic politician, provide both inspiration and cause for gratitude: What would we do without them? The Church in English-speaking Canada, much like the Catholic Church in England, depends on converts for a great deal of her evangelical energy.

Without converts my life and priesthood would be significantly different and considerably poorer. I have had the joy of welcoming coverts to the Catholic Church, and once, before my ordination, of sponsoring a friend upon his reception. Stanislaus du Plessis, a South African Calvinist of formidable intelligence and indefatigable in argument, was my closest friend when I was studying at Cambridge. Into the early hours of the morning he would engage me in religious disputes, probing my apologetics for this or that aspect of the Catholic faith. Eventually I would ask him what it was that I could say that would just allow me to go home to bed; so persistent was he that I was tempted to abjure my faith just to earn respite!

In the end, there were no words of mine that could satisfy him. Only the Word would suffice, and a few years afterwards he found his way into the Catholic Church, where he found that Word, and where that Word found him. In the beginning was the Word, Saint John tells us, and at the beginning of every conversion story is that same Word. The many words that follow in this book remind us that the Word still searches for souls – and finds them.

As a university chaplain, I daily encounter on campus those who are searching and who desire deeply to be found by the One whom they know is searching for them. The stories in this book will be for them and those similarly situated a measure of hope, a portion of wisdom, and an instrument of grace.

**Father Raymond J. de Souza**
**Wolfe Island, Ontario**
**July 2009**

# Conrad Black

**Conrad Black was born in Montreal in 1944. He is a financier and former investor and newspaper publisher; he founded the National Post in 1998, and was the Chairman of the London (UK) Daily Telegraphy from 1998 to 2004. He has published biographies of Quebec Premier Maurice Duplessis, as well as of Presidents Richard Nixon and Franklin D. Roosevelt. He is currently a columnist for the National Post.**

# Rome after All!

My religious upbringing was casually Protestant, a respect for Christian tradition and high religious tolerance, but no encouragement to be a practicing or seriously believing Christian. Something like this was the condition of most of my relatives and school and social contemporaries in Toronto and elsewhere in English-speaking Canada. My family was divided between atheism and agnosticism, and I followed rather unthinkingly and inactively in those paths into my twenties. When I moved to Quebec in 1966, I was astounded by the omnipresence there of Roman Catholicism.

I studied the law, language, and history of Quebec, and eventually produced a lengthy biography of Maurice L. Duplessis, Quebec's longest serving and most controversial leader, and became an official of Paul-Emile Cardinal Leger's charity, (he was the archbishop of Montreal from 1950 to 1967). This organization, Le Cardinal Leger et ses Oeuvres, built a modern hospital in the Cameroons, where the cardinal had moved in 1967.

In my Duplessis research, I steeped myself in the relations of Church and state in traditional Quebec, and interviewed many prominent clergymen apart from Leger. I had had the usual English-Canadian view that the Church had allied itself with reactionary political elements to slow the progress of Quebec and keep it in superstitious retardation. There certainly had been reactionary, and even racist and quasi-fascist elements in the Quebec clergy, but they never predominated.

My research revealed that only the Church had sustained the French language in Quebec, the demographic survival of French Canadians, and the prevalence of literacy, provision of health care, and even most capital formation, (as in the Caisses Populaires Desjardins credit unions attached to almost every parish), for nearly two centuries after the Battle of the Plains of Abraham in 1759.

I met the founder of the cooperation movement, the Dominican Georges-Henri Levesque, and other prominent figures in social organizations, including the Jesuit Emile Bouvier of the Institute of Industrial relations. (Duplessis had told my eventual friend Malcolm Muggeridge that the secret to governing Quebec was to keep the Dominicans and Jesuits quarrelling with each other.) In general, the

16

clerical personnel were at least as impressive as their secular analogues.

I was impressed by the worldliness of such a spiritual organization. Leger was always mindful of the importance of money, but was no less a man of dedicated spirituality for that. It was a cultural eye-opener for me to see how official Catholicism tried to quantify or at least aggregate factors that I had not thought susceptible to such precise calibration. Official summaries of the lives of saints customarily ended: "Thus glorified by evident signs and miracles, he/she is numbered among the Church's saints," as if having filled out a behavioural scorecard. Far from being an empire of hocus-pocus and mesmerisation of the primitive, of exploitation, hypocrisy, reaction, and ever proliferating poverty, I saw the Roman Catholic Church in Quebec and later in most other places, as fiercely dedicated to the kingdom of God, resistant to opportunistic fads, concerned to modernize without eroding faith, armed with intellectual arguments quite equal, at the least, to those of their secular opponents or rivals, and almost always a champion of human rights when it wasn't in common cause with less altruistic elements against the Antichrist of communism.

Of course, Quebec had been a priest-ridden society, with a great deal of meddlesome, priggish excess, but with all the secularization that has occurred in Quebec, relatively few problems of deviant behaviour have been unearthed or even alleged.

Duplessis had told Leger, (the cardinal said to me one evening at his mission near Yaounde), that "If you squeeze a fish hard enough, it will get

17

away." Leger said that he had replied that he was well aware of that but that it was Duplessis who was exploiting the paranoia of the rural bishops by fanning their fears that any move to secularization would bring down Satanism and assimilation on French Canada.

This discussion took place on the veranda of his pre-World War I German mission where he lived, near the clinic that cared for destitute lepers and other wretchedly disadvantaged people. The numbers and courage of Roman Catholic missions and clinics assisting the most distressed people in the world is an under-recognized, large-scale devolution of faithful people to the most challenging causes. Dozens of them are murdered every year and for all of them, their work is its reward. For every Mother Theresa, there are dozens of other, similarly inspired, selfless, and effective people. It is hard not to be affected and uplifted by their devotion.

The almost exclusive Church provision of education and health care to French Quebec was overly prolonged and averse to competition, but the resulting savings in salarial costs of teachers and nurses enabled the government of Quebec to devote most of its budget to what is now called infrastructure. Duplessis built thousands of schools, the new campuses of Laval and Montreal Universities, the University of Sherbrooke, hundreds of hospitals and clinics, thousands of miles of roads, the first Canadian autoroutes, and he brought electricity to 97% of rural Quebec. Quebec was even a pioneer in disability pensions and day care. From 1944 to

Duplessis's death in 1959 was the only time when Quebec's economic growth exceeded English Canada's.

Public works and social programs in Quebec in the fifties may not seem to have much to do with the merits of Catholicism, (despite Duplessis's hilarious campaign against the Liberal federal government's importation of "Communist eggs" from Poland in 1956), but both the episcopate and the lower clergy were essential associates in these years of swift social and economic progress.

When I was familiarizing myself with all this, Leger had gone to Africa, Duplessis's Union Nationale was extinct, Quebec had become wildly secular, and M. Laliberté, the head of the Quebec Teachers' Union, opened his 1975 annual convention with a panegyric of joy at the "liberation" of South Vietnam. French Canada had secularized itself, as English Canada had urged and wanted, (though that is not why it did it). Now the same people were performing the same educational and paramedical tasks in the same buildings for the same population at ten times the cost to the Quebec taxpayers, and were frequently on strike, as taxes and debt soared, the birth rate collapsed, the separatists advanced, and the cultural rights of the non-French were redefined as "revocable privileges." The fish, indeed, had got away.

The Church was in steep decline in Quebec, but this was no less interesting a perspective for appreciating its strengths. As when it was at its height, the quality of its subsequent leaders, Cardinals Ouellet and Turcotte, is rather more evident than the merit of corresponding secular leaders, although their dominion has shrunk and the province of the state has grown, comparative to the times of Leger and Duplessis, or the prior epoch when the Taschereau family produced the cardinal, the premier, and the chief justices.

Now the impecunious parishes, scanty congregations, and the apparent anachronism of the contemporary Church seemed to produce a sharp division between those clergy buoyed by the challenge, feeling themselves like the Dark Ages' monks squatting in forests and on mountain tops, agents of spiritual and cultural preservation, and those who were just the detritus of the Old Church, parched, wizened, and passing slowly on.

In Quebec as in France, those who persist in the practice of the faith are not the oldest, poorest, most desperate, though those are there, but they are a very random group, including elegant young women, evidently successful men, bright students, unselfconscious, curious, and assured. The spiritual edifice of the Church functions obliviously to market share, and there is a common strain of intelligent and hopeful faith, regardless of fashion, age, or economics. Whether in packed and mighty St. Peter's Basilica or St. Patrick's Cathedral (New York), in a simple wooden building like the Indian church in Sept-Iles, Quebec, in primitive religious structures in the Cameroons, at fashionable resorts like Biarritz, St. Jean Cap Ferrat, Portofino, or even Palm Beach, or in the improvised chapel in my prison as I write, there is a discernible, but almost inexpressible denominator that unites communicants. I am still impressed by the purposeful spring in the step of people approaching a Catholic Church as the hour of a service peels.

It may be that I was startled to discover this because I was so accustomed from my early years to think of Protestantism, except for the evangelicals, as conditional and tentative, protesting, after all, against the worldliness of Rome. When I first went to Rome, in 1963, I had just read a description of John Updike's in the New Yorker of his first visit to St. Peter's, in which he was so astounded by the grandeur of the Basilica, by its size, solidity, magnificence, architectural genius and collections of high art, that he felt compelled to add his name to thousands of others written in the graffiti in the wall of the curved stairway to the cupola, 44 stories above the ground, (in a building constructed continuously between the 15$^{th}$ and 18$^{th}$ centuries.)

I dimly and roughly remembered Byron's: "Worthiest of God, the holy and the true...Majesty, power, glory, strength and beauty, all are aisled in this eternal ark of worship undefiled." It was hard not to see what he meant.

The sense of indulgent receptivity of this incomparable building was somehow emphasized by its ostentatious affordability of indifference to those who would come as sceptics or antagonists. Unlike the Pyramids, the Great Wall, Angkor Wat, or even the Kremlin, there is nothing Ozymandean about it. Unlike the Pentagon, it is completely human, while inciting divine contemplation. My visits to Lourdes and Fatima in the ensuing couple of years revealed concepts of mass faith in the miraculous, scientifically attested to, that were also amazing to a former spiritually slumbering Protestant, and difficult to ignore or discount.

These are just fragments of background to set the perspective from which I approached Catholicism. By the time I left Quebec in 1974 and returned to Toronto, I was satisfied that there were spiritual forces in the world, and that it was possible, occasionally and unpredictably, to gain something enlightening and even inspiriting from them. I had begun to pray at the end of each day, developing my own groping formulations of worship, and feeling no compulsion to join formal religious practice, but curious about where this might lead.

I had stepped on to the escalator, and knew from reading of famous converts, especially Cardinal Newman and Cardinal Manning, G.K. Chesterton, Oscar Wilde, Evelyn Waugh, Siegfried Sassoon, Graham Greene, Muriel Spark, Malcolm Muggeridge, Frank and Elizabeth Longford, Orestes Brownson and some less famous people, including contributors to this book, that it was likely to end in Rome.

Wherever it might lead, I was determined not to move a millimetre until I was convinced that it was justified by belief. There would be no surrender to momentum or the fatigue of argument. But I had discovered by my early thirties that I no longer had any confidence in the non-existence of God. It was more of an intellectual and a psychological strain not to believe in God than to believe, and not from the impulse of hopefulness; from the impossibility of shutting out spirituality, abandoning curiosity about getting to grips with the infinite, before the beginning and after the end of time, and beyond the outer limits of space. Logically, there is some sort of organizing principle abroad, or at least something unexplained, partially defining, and at least slightly accessible.

Whether it was Bismarck speaking of "listening for God's footfall and touching the hem of His garment as He passes," or Britain's late Cardinal Hume saying it was "like a screen. You can detect something behind it but can't make out clearly what it is," simply dismissing religious belief is not like dismissing astrology or chiropractic, or eschewing mushrooms.

This is the only possible route to some insights beyond the normally discernible. Declining any interest in it, I gradually discovered, was an unjustifiable reduction of my modest intellectual canvass.

I read a good deal of the most admired arguments in support of God's existence, especially Aquinas and Newman, and many of the more familiar or florid against, such as Ingersoll and Marx. My favourite of this latter group was a humorously vituperative Welshman named Powys, who claimed to have "heard the Hazzan chanted from the minarets in the blazing mid-day sun, and seen the African in his rain-forest, the men of China, raising sinew-lean arms to the heavens...It has never availed."

On the other side, I could never say, and cannot now, as Newman did, that "I am as sure of the existence of God as I am of my own hands and feet."

Newman's most picaresque argument, valuable for its almost impish wit, was the quotation of Napoleon, near the end at St. Helena, from the not entirely reliable Lacordaire, at the end of Newman's tour de force, *A Grammar of Assent*.

Napoleon was introduced as "the great man who so influenced the destinies of the nations of Europe at the start of this century." Lacordaire wrote that Napoleon had mused: Someone who

> died a miscreant's death eighteen hundred years ago, whose likeness is displayed in the principal squares of great cities, at rural crossways, in palaces and in hovels, before the new born and the failing vision of those about to die; effortlessly achieved what Alexander and Caesar and I did not begin to accomplish. Can he be less than divine, one to whom our eyes turn, as to a father and a God?

Of course, the answer to Napoleon's question is yes, he might not be divine on that evidence alone, but the alleged fact that he posed it at all is of interest. Napoleon was not an atheist, any more than Alexander or Caesar were; rather they saw themselves as God's lieutenants, or even duumvirs. Caesar had himself proclaimed a deity, so he could scarcely claim there were none already. Napoleon, nephew of Cardinal Retz, said: "Of course the people must have their religion, and of course the state must control it." Even Hitler and Stalin were not atheists. Hitler was a pagan who detested Christianity. Indeed, what he considered the Jews' botch of the disposal of Christ, the ignorance of the Sanhedrin and the mindless barbarity of the Jewish mobs, chanting "Crucify him!" and "Give us Barabbas," to which he imputed the rise of Christianity, is one of the few slightly plausible explanations of his otherwise inexplicable anti-Semitism. This was his perverse version of the legend of the Christ-killers, mutated from the traditional grievance against messianicide into the bungled elimination of a subversive troublemaker. Hitler seems to have believed in some quasi-Wagnerian notion of a god of war, more formidable than the vacillating, hag-ridden, and generally un-Godlike Wotan of the Ring of the Niebelungen.

Even Stalin, expelled from the seminary as he had been, and leader of the world's atheistic Marxists, believed in God, though he thought him an opponent, and thought himself a sort of leader of the opposition. He said to the film director, Sergei Eisenstein, of his film, Ivan the Terrible, "God hindered the Czar Ivan in his work." Stalin was creating a "new man" through social engineering, a man superior to the one inherited from God, and perfectible, in the pursuit of which objective, Stalin blithely murdered tens of millions of them.

I had no difficulty discarding the scientific claims of people like Bertrand Russell, that there was a finite amount of knowledge in the universe, and that every day we more closely approached a plenitude of knowledge. It seemed to me that the greatest discoveries, remarkable as they were, did just the opposite. The revolution of the earth around the sun, like the process of evolution, diminished us, as less prominent in the universe and descended from a lower order of animals. The fact that we can't control our sub-consciousness does not make us more redoubtable, but more vulnerable. And atomic energy enhances the prospects for human self-destruction, at least as much as positive applications of it.

The exaggerated claims of the scientists were not much more persuasive than the similarly overblown liberties of the miraculists and creationists. At some point, science and revelation intersect, and faith is no natural enemy of scholarship.

I read many of the more accessible Catholic writers, especially Newman, Aquinas, St. Augustine, and Maritain. And when Gerald Emmett Carter became the archbishop of Toronto, in 1979, I quickly became an acquaintance, then a friend, and eventually an intimate. He never pressed his religious views or attempted to proselytize, any more than Cardinal Leger had. He too, became a cardinal, in 1980. I frequently stopped at his house, in Rosedale, on my way uptown from my office, and we discussed a good many subjects, sometimes including ecclesiastical ones, usually over some of his very good claret. These were tumultuous years in my commercial, and at times, personal life also. His counsel was only given when requested and was always wise. (When he retired as archbishop, he became a director of one of our companies, Argus Corporation, and, even in this field and at his age, his opinions were useful.) Despite the gap in our ages of more than thirty years, no one ever had a truer, or more valued friend than he was to me.

From the early seventies to the mid-eighties, I approached Rome at a snail's pace. Having concluded that God existed, I could not seriously entertain the thought of not trying to be in contact with Him. And since I believed in general and prayed to and worshipped Him, it was not long before I wished to do so in some framework, to benefit from accumulated wisdom and traditions and from a community of faith.

It was not especially challenging, given my light Protestant upbringing, to stay in the Christian tradition. From all accounts, Christ appeared to be a divinely inspired person, in traditional parlance, a divine. There was no reason to doubt that he told St. Peter to found a church. I had never much doubted that, whatever its "inanities, fatuities, and compromises," (a quote from Leger), the Roman Catholic Church was the premier Christian church.

I read a good deal of Christian history and while the financial corruption of the medieval Church was frequently outrageous, and the Papacy was at times batted about like a badminton bird by the great Roman families, the Church seems to have performed its pastoral functions well enough, or it would not have survived at all. Its intellectual life was vigorous and was not seriously challenged by the Reformationists. It had performed its role as a conservator of Western culture and civilization; a large part of the extravagance objected to was devoted to the promotion of the arts and the flowering of the Renaissance, especially the 220-year construction of St. Peter's.

The congregational churches that sprang up in the Reformation always seemed to me the ecclesiastical equivalent of people approving their own expense accounts, as the clergy could be revoked by their ostensible followers. Whatever the benevolence of the Protestant churches and the frailties of Rome, the fragmentation of Christianity among self-directed national sects never seemed to me consistent with Christ's instruction to St. Peter to found and lead a universal church.

As a nominal Anglican, I had always had some problems with Henry VIII as a religious leader. That he apostatised to facilitate marriage with a woman whom he soon beheaded on false charges of adultery, seized the monasteries to finance his wars in France, and required his puppet parliament to give him back the title "Defender of the Faith," (still on the Canadian coinage in honour of the present Queen), that the pope had given him in recognition of a canonical paper Erasmus had ghost-written for him, never filled me with confidence in the legitimacy of the Church of England. More and Fisher were more morally compelling figures than the Henricians, and many of Britain's great pre-Wren Anglican churches were seized from Rome.

Nor was I convinced that the replacement of the Stuarts with the House of Orange, was the "Glorious Revolution" MacAulay and the Trevelyans and other talented Whig myth-makers have claimed. James II was a blundering monarch, but his Toleration Act, promising religious freedom for Jews, Roman Catholics, disestablished Protestants and non-believers, was not subversive or ignoble, and was a shabby pretext for a revolution. The Anglicans, as Newman had written, had an impressive lower clergy, but it seemed more, (to me), a measure of well-placed cultural and ethnic faith in the British and American upper classes and institutions, and a contingent, sectarian insurance policy, than the earthly portal to the kingdom of God. The Anglicans have never really decided whether they are Protestant or Catholic, only that they "don't Pope," though even that wavers from time to time.

Luther, though formidable and righteous, was less appealing to me than both the worldly Romans, tinged with rascality though they were, and the leading Papist zealots of the Counter-Reformation. The Jesuits and Capucins had to be more thoughtful and less Teutonically joyless than Luther, a Bismarckian iron chancellor unleavened by a cynical wit.

The serious followers of Calvin, Dr. Knox, and Wesley were, to me, too puritanical, but also too barricaded into ethnic and cultural fastnesses, too much the antithesis of universalism and of the often flawed, yet grand Roman effort to reconcile the spiritual and the material, without corrupting the first and squandering the second.

There was something warmly reassuring, as well as amusingly knowledgeable, about Duplessis's explanation to Leger, (told to me by both the cardinal and Duplessis's very long-serving assistant, Aurea Cloutier), that:

> We are like the Brueghel triptych in the Louvre, where you and I sit in the centre panel surrounded by pomp and ceremony, conducting our offices, while sexual orgies and drunken debauchery flourish in one side-panel, and people are picking pockets and taking bribes in the other. We maintain appearances, but we know how the world functions. You encourage the

people to behave better, and I have to prosecute them
when they commit outrages, but we are dealing with
people in a world we know too well.

Leger did not strenuously demur. It isn't reform-
ist zeal, but it is grounded in experience, is melior-
ist, and has attainable objectives. And it was Catholicism in Quebec, an endearing blend of idealism
and cynicism. Fanatics are very tiresome, and usually enjoy the fate of Haman in the book of Esther;
of Savonarola, Robespierre, Trotsky, Goebbels, and
Guevara.

Islam was out of the question; too anti-Western,
too identified with the thirteenth century-decline
and contemporary belligerency of the Arabs; and
the Koran is alarmingly violent, even compared to
the Old Testament. Judaism, though close theologically, is more tribal and philosophical than spiritual.
And it was the spiritual bait that I sought, that converted me from atheism, that I premeditatedly swal-
lowed, and that prompted me to agitate the line and
be reeled in by the Fisher of Souls. I thought it more
likely that the 80% of the early Jews who became
Christians, starting with Christ, had correctly identified the Messiah than that the proverbially "stiff-
necked" rump of continuing Jewry are right still,
ostensibly, to be waiting for Him.

It need hardly be said that the Jews are the chosen people of the Old Testament, that they have
made a huge contribution to civilization, and that
they have been horribly persecuted. But being Jewish today, apart from the orthodox, is more of an
exclusive society, and a tradition of oppression and
survival, than an accessible faith.

The Eastern religions, to the very slight degree that I have studied them, are philosophical guides to living, not frameworks for the existence and purpose of man. In terms of real religious affiliation for me, it was Rome or nothing. To exercise and explore my faith, I would have to chin myself on Catholic dogma, at least up to a threshold I had not approached before. I was satisfied, from my reading, and from my visits to Lourdes and Fatima, that miracles do sometimes occur. Therefore, logically, any miracle could occur, even the most apparently challenging, such as the Virgin Birth and the physical Ascension of Christ.

In the spring of 1986, Cardinal Carter asked me my religious beliefs. I recited my plodding baby-steps on the ladder: there were spiritual aspects to life that were not mere superstition, and that constituted or at least evidenced God; that Christ was divinely inspired, had told St. Peter to found a Church, and that the legitimate continuator of that Church was Roman Catholicism. I desired to be in communion with God, and accepted that the surest means of doing so, though not sure, and not the only one, was as a communicant in the Roman Catholic Church.

I believed that miracles occurred, though I couldn't attest to particular ones, that given the wonders of creation and of the infinite, and the imperfections of man, we all properly belonged, frequently, on our knees before an effigy of the Creator or his professed and acclaimed son, and that sincere and concentrated worship could be enlightening. I also, like Chesterton and countless millions of others, wished some method of being "rid of my sins," as I agree with Newman that "Our conscience is God speaking within us." The Cardinal replied that I was "at the door," but that the one point I had to embrace if I wished to enter, and without which, all Christianity, he boldly asserted, "is a fraud and a trumpery," was the Resurrection of Christ. If I believed that, I was eligible; if I did not, I wasn't. What he was asking was not unreasonable, and I reflected on it a few minutes and concluded that since, as defined, I believed in God and in miracles, I could at least suppress doubt sufficiently to meet his criterion. I considered it a little longer to be sure that I wasn't allowing momentum, contemplative fatigue, or my great regard for him to push me over the finish line.

After a silence of perhaps five minutes, I said that I thought I could clear that hurdle. He asked me if I wished to be received. I did, and was, in the chapel in his home a few days later, June 18, 1986. I thought of Pascal's attribution to Christ: "You would not have sought me if you had not already found me," and of the statement by, I think, one of the saints, that "All the way to God is God, because Christ said: 'I am the way.'"

I have taken the sacraments at least once a week since, and have confessed when I feel sinful. This is not an overly frequent sensation, but when it occurs, I can again agree with Newman that our consciences are "powerful, peremptory, unargumentative, irrational, minatory and definitive." The strain of trying to ignore or restrain an aroused conscience can be intolerable. Confession and repentance, if sincere, is easier, more successful, and more creditable.

Though there are many moments of scepticism as matters arise, and the dark nights of the soul that seem to assail almost everyone, visit me too, I have never had anything remotely resembling a lapse, nor a sense of forsakenness, even when I was unjustly indicted, convicted, and imprisoned, in a country I formerly much admired.

Confidence that there is at least some sort of an organizing principle in the world, the experience that worship sometimes produces enhanced understanding of my travails and observations; and some metaphysical background, do provide a hinterland for perceptions, and with it, relative serenity and proportionality, even, and perhaps especially, in times of extreme tension, poignancy, and adversity. And there have been some.

My life-long tolerance of all creeds, including impassioned atheism, has not abated. I feel no more desire than I ever did to judge, asperse, or scold. In religion as in some other matters, I will not presume to advise, but am, up to a point, prepared to say what I am doing and why, if anyone is curious. In the matters described here, I have had no regrets or any unanswerable second thoughts.

# Kathy Clark

**Kathy Clark was born in Budapest, Hungary, in 1953. In 1956 her parents fled the revolution-torn country, leaving her in the care of her grandparents. After a six and a half year wait, Kathy immigrated to Canada to be reunited with her parents in Toronto. Her first year in Canada is the background for her first novel, *A Whisper in My Heart*. Her other books include *Guardian Angel House*. She is the founder of Chilawee Trails Camp for girls. Kathy and her husband Bruce live in Kanata. They have six children and three grandchildren.**

## Led by Love

My conversion from Judaism to Catholicism was not brought about by any sudden or miraculous revelation. Rather it was the result of years of searching and questioning with my heart and mind for that elusive power which, I sensed from a very early age, constantly surrounded me.

Ever since I can remember, I knew that I was loved. I do not mean this in the normal sense of a child being loved by her parents. In fact, that form of human, unconditional love was not part of my experience. My parents fled revolution-torn Hungary in 1956, leaving me behind, at the age of two and a half, in the care of my grandparents. My parents' hopes of sending for me as soon as they settled in a safe country were dashed when the Communist government closed the Hungarian borders. It was six and a half years before I was re-united with my parents in Canada.

Though life with my grandparents was comfortable and loving enough, I always knew that I was missing something. I resented my parents for having left me behind. But more than this, during those early years of my childhood, I was subjected to several physically and psychologically abusive situations.

Yet in all of this, I had a supernatural sense that I was loved. I was convinced that there was some force out there that loved me. This was not just childish wistful thinking. It was a certainty that led me in my growing years and through adolescence and early adulthood to search constantly for the source of that love.

My grandparents were not very religious. My grandmother lit the Sabbath candles and we celebrated the major Holidays of Rosh Hashanah, Yom Kippur and Passover, but there was little talk of God and I was seldom encouraged to pray. My childish conception of God was of some unknowable being who was often displeased with me but who might grant me some of my wishes if I asked.

This was very different from my sense of a loving, caring power that was aware of all my thoughts and feelings. Even when I knew I was wilfully disobedient, I also knew that this 'power' as I conceived it, still loved me and understood my weakness. When I was very young, I thought that perhaps it was my favourite doll that had some magical powers to emanate love and comfort. Later, when I discovered fairy tales, I thought that perhaps it was in them that the secret of the 'power' lay. I read every fairy tale I could get my hands on, asking my grandmother to get me newer books from the store or library. I was convinced that the secret of the universe was hidden between the lines of these stories. Needless to say, they never satisfied my desire. I met with disappointment.

In 1963, at the age of ten, I came to Canada to live with my parents. Our first few years together were turbulent, but again, I knew that there was someone greater who loved me. My parents were even less 'religious' than my grandparents. My mother only lit the Sabbath candles sporadically, and we went to the Synagogue twice a year on the high holidays. These events were more of a social occasion than a spiritual one. Celebrating my Bat mitzvah at the age of twelve was not much different from an elaborate birthday party, with an added discomfort: having to dress up and recite a speech in Hebrew in front of a large group of people.

As I entered my late teens, I acknowledged that 'God' was the appropriate label for the source of the love I had experienced throughout my life. But I still didn't know what God was truly like or how to connect with him other than just feeling his loving presence. We lived in a Jewish neighbourhood and most of my friends in high school were Jewish.

Though their families observed the major holidays more seriously than mine did, my friends all regarded Judaism as a cultural rather than a religious reality. I had a few non-Jewish friends, but whatever religious background they had, it did not profoundly affect their daily lives. While we spoke intellectually of God and the meaning of life, we didn't seek guidance from a specific religion. The main value of Christianity and Judaism for us was in the cultural symbolism they provided in art and literature.

My personal search for the nature of God continued in a haphazard way. I explored some of the ideas of Buddhism, read books by the mystic Gurdjieff, books on Sufism, I read the I Ching – the Chinese book of changes, and attended Gnostic and Hare Krishna prayer/meditation sessions. While some of these groups held my interest longer than others, eventually I found that they did not adequately explain the reason behind my certainty that I was individually loved. The God I was looking for knew me, and therefore everyone else, personally. At the same time, He was somehow mysteriously present in all of creation around me. Sometimes my longing for true knowledge of God became very painful, reducing me to tears. He seemed so close and yet so far away.

Without giving it much thought or knowing anything specific about it, I rejected Christianity. I assumed that it must be much like the Judaism that I was familiar with – a set of rules and rituals without any spiritual depth.

All this searching took place in the late sixties and early seventies, the Hippie years. Like many of my generation, I was inclined to disdain the pronouncements of traditional authority and felt that I could find a better path on my own. Thankfully, there were many things I avoided or refused to try simply because everybody else did them. I was determined to choose my own way. I wanted to be completely free.

In 1973 I registered in the Environmental Studies program at the University of Waterloo. There I met Bruce Clark, now my husband. He had been raised in a fundamentalist Protestant religion called Brethren. While he did not adhere to all the teachings of this sect, he took the Bible very seriously. Bruce was a student of psychology and philosophy, and we had many very interesting discussions. The only area where I considered him very close-minded was with respect to religion. I could not believe that in the society we lived in, he still thought that those 'archaic' moral standards set forth in the Bible were valid. It was a constant source of disagreement between us. He knew of my search for this loving 'power' behind the universe and tried to tell me about Christianity, but I only saw a list of 'do's and don'ts in what he had to say. I pointed out that his list was little different from the ones my parents had tried to instil in me. I considered them a product of the social structure that preached them. Other societies, other cultures, other times had different rules. I had not yet found anything that I considered basic and fundamental to all of humanity. I believed we could make up our own rules, as long as living by those rules did not hurt others.

At the end of my first year of Environmental Studies, I decided to see Canada, and travelled to the Rocky Mountains to work for the summer. After one month, I became restless with my job at a local hotel in Jasper, and quit in order to explore the rest of the country. I felt that I was learning more from real life now than I did at University and therefore decided not to go back. I travelled to Vancouver Island working along the way, then headed to the Maritimes. The onset of cold weather in October and my desire to see Bruce again, finally drove me back to a more sheltered life in Ontario. I worked for a few months, long enough to re-connect with Bruce and make some money to finance my next trip.

Before I left, I decided to sit in on one of Bruce's philosophy classes. It was a class taught at St. Jerome's College, a Catholic subsidiary of the University of Waterloo. Bruce often talked of this one professor, Dr. Gerry Campbell, because of his giftedness as a teacher and the interesting discussions they always had in class. My curiosity was aroused. I wanted to hear Dr. Campbell myself.

I arrived at the class slightly late. As I opened the door, Dr. Campbell, with his commanding voice, was reading from the beginning of Aristotle's Metaphysics.

"All men by nature desire to know." The power of those words struck me. I instinctively recognized their truth since the desire for knowledge was so strong in me. Throughout my school years, from the

earliest grades, I had gotten into the habit of reviewing each night the new things I had learned that day
– not academic things, but rather, truths or insights
about life and relationships.

In recognizing the truth of the statement that 'all
men by nature desire to know' I was struck by the
concept of nature itself. The very way in which we
were made, our human nature, dictated what was
right for us as humans. Therefore, there must be a
way that all people were meant to be. For the first
time I gave credence to the idea that there might be
an objective right or wrong way for us to behave.
Perhaps others had tried to tell me this before, but
due to either their presentation or my obstinacy, I
had never understood.

For someone who has not grown up in that era
or who hasn't experienced the burden of complete
but directionless freedom, it might be difficult to
appreciate the relief that I felt at finally realizing
that there was truly a right and wrong. It was all a
part of human nature. I could come to understand
what it was. There was a general law that applied to
all people, meaning that I did not have to be constantly preoccupied with what was the right thing
for me to do in this moment based on how I felt.
How I felt continually changed, but this law was a
constant against which I could evaluate my feelings
and thoughts.

I wanted to learn more from Dr. Campbell and
before I left for Israel at the beginning of March, I
registered at Waterloo again for the fall semester,
this time in a joint Environmental Studies / Philosophy program.

My decision to go to Israel had little to do with my Jewish roots. I went because I knew that apart from my airfare, I would have virtually no expenses as a volunteer working on a Kibbutz. Kibbutz Geva was located between the town of Affula and the Sea of Galilee and just an hour's hike across the hills to the town of Nazareth. The kibbutz was a rather affluent one and they treated their volunteers well. I enjoyed my outdoor job, picking grapefruits for six hours a day. On weekends, I went on excursions to Nazareth, Galilee, Jerusalem, Haifa and other places of interest. Towards the end of my stay, the kibbutz financed a ten day excursion in the Negev Desert for its volunteers. Because of my obstinate refusal to give any consideration to Judaism or Christianity, I avoided all the regular places of interest in these locations. I did not visit any of the major religious attractions. Yet, in this ancient land, I could not escape the sense of awe and holiness that seemed to permeate the very ground beneath my feet. My longing to get to know God intensified. I kept a journal in which I wrote these two poems which give a good sense of my state of mind at the time:

## Goodnight Jerusalem

Trying to get
So much living
In movement, chaos,
Faking life's intensity.
Round and round in a circle you spin;
Well, have you broken through the wall?
Are you in?
Have you touched that secret?

41

You're sure it's hidden somewhere…
Someone must see the truth;
Someone can surely take you there;
Maybe in another town,
Maybe on another face, Maybe…
But can't stop now,
Must keep going,
Surely the time is soon,
For you've read all the sacred books,
You've gone the way of the fool.
Then why the empty laughter
As you turn to gaze at the sky?
The sun sends out its warmth,
Caresses the fear inside.
You're just a lonesome traveler,
The hobo of the soul,
Living on stolen dreams,
Kicking the dust of the road.
Good night Jerusalem.

## Jerusalem

Kneeling,
On the sacred sands of time
You wonder at the secrets
That you know you'll never find.
The tower raised to greatness,
The poems written in praise,
the offering of jewels;
None reveal the game
That men of old invented
To lead you through this maze.
The truth to them was simple
For it bore a human face.

By the end of May, I again grew restless. I missed Bruce and decided to return to Waterloo.

In September, the first course I took with Dr. Campbell was on the Nichomachean Ethics of Aristotle. Through it, I gained a better understanding of human nature, our sense of right and wrong and how to determine how we ought to act. What struck me in particular was the certainty and confidence with which Dr. Campbell approached the whole subject. I was taking another ethics course at the same time on the main Waterloo campus, in which the professor refused to pass judgement either on the various modern philosophers we studied or on our own views of right and wrong. It was a very frustrating class.

Dr. Campbell's classes frequently continued after the allotted time. Often, after an evening lecture he would proceed with several of his students to a local pub where our discussions in philosophy and theology would continue into the early hours of the morning. Dr. Campbell was Catholic, and his faith permeated most of our discussions especially since Bruce was getting very interested in the compatibility between philosophy and Catholicism. We had many questions and Dr. Campbell patiently answered them all. There were even a few times when after the pub closed, he would invite us back to his home where his wife Martha would get out of bed and cheerfully serve us fresh homemade muffins and hot chocolate as if she did this all the time at 3:00am.

Even with my increased understanding of human nature and our sense of right and wrong, my conversations with Bruce often degenerated into arguments. I liked him very much, but I considered his Christian faith a serious obstacle in our relationship. As the school year came to an end, and I had more time, I decided to read the New Testament. I figured that this would help me to understand where Bruce was coming from, and help me to better argue against him. In addition, it would help me to understand all the connections Dr. Campbell made between the New Testament and the philosophy of Aristotle and Thomas Aquinas.

I bought a Bible and almost every morning of that summer, before I started into my day, I spent about an hour reading the Gospels on the small balcony of my apartment. Throughout the summer months, Bruce and I kept in touch with Dr. Campbell, who by now was not just a teacher but also a friend. We met regularly for philosophical discussions in which, Dr. Campbell often pointed out the rational nature of the Catholic Church. While I did not at first let on that I was reading the New Testament, (I didn't want them to think that I was caving in) these discussions helped fill in many gaps in my knowledge of the bible and in turn, my readings helped me to understand what Dr. Campbell and Bruce were talking about.

As I read through the gospels of Mathew, Mark and Luke, I grew fascinated with the person of Jesus. Reluctantly I conceded that he must have been a very impressive man. I liked his stories, his gentleness and humility. I was upset by how badly he was treated even though he only tried to do good. I especially liked his compassion for the outcasts of society. If only he were alive now, I thought, he would understand me. He would be someone I could talk with very sincerely, and not be afraid of being judged.

And then, I came to the Gospel of St. John.

From the previous gospels, I learned of the person of Jesus – of who he was as a man and what he said and did. Because of my trip to Israel, I could clearly picture the physical environment that he lived in. I imagined him walking in the white rock strewn hills of Judea or along the shores of the Sea of Galilee. I regretted now that I had refused to enter any of the religious buildings associated with his time on earth.

The gospel of St. John provided a spiritual depth and mystical perspective of Jesus' mission on earth. I had not noticed this in the other gospels. Before the gospel of John, I thought of Jesus as a very interesting man – one that I felt I would have admired and would have loved to speak with. As I read the gospel of John it finally dawned on me that Jesus was claiming to be the son of God; of being one with God. And that, if we believed that he was who he said he was, and did the things he told us to do, then we too could enter into this intimate union with God. Jesus' main message of love and forgiveness, his constant emphasis on God's mercy, were the very things I had been searching for. His description of God as a loving father who was waiting for us to find him was what I had been experiencing for most of my life. While there were many things I did not understand, I felt the truth of this fundamental message with my heart.

For the first time I also seriously considered the prospect of everlasting life from a Christian perspective. It struck me that Jesus actually claimed to rise from the dead; that heaven existed and that the way we lived our lives made a difference as to whether we would get there or not. All this was very different from the accounts of re-incarnation or the vague oneness of spirits that I had previously encountered in the religions and cults I had previously explored. I was attracted by this everlasting view of life that Jesus presented. I hoped that it was true. If it was true, I realized, it would give a completely new depth of significance to my life on earth.

By now, it was the beginning of August and I left on a pre-planned, weeklong hike with a friend along the Bruce Peninsula. After the first couple of days of hiking over rough terrain with heavy packs on our backs and camping out at night, my friend had had enough, and returned home. I continued alone, glad of the solitude to sort through all my conflicting thoughts and feelings. The breathtaking natural environment, the physical exertion of each day and the simple but nourishing meals I prepared, all helped to make that week a deeply reflective one. I thought over all that I had read in the gospels balanced against the discussions with Dr. Campbell. It was clear to me now that God was not just a laid-back source of love, but had actively created all the beauty around me as well as my individual soul with a particular purpose. If he could do all this, then why not also will himself to take on human form in order to more effectively bring people into union with himself. The history of humanity showed that on our own we floundered in uncertainty. All the various religions I had so far examined were an indication of that.

With my new-found understanding of God, I often felt that he was right there with me as I struggled up rocky cliffs or splashed barefoot through a shallow stream.

At the end of the week, I boarded a bus to return to Waterloo. As I neared the city, I knew that I did not want to return to my life the way it had been. I wanted to change; to overcome some of the bad habits and destructive lifestyles I had struggled with for years. While before I had felt that God loved me through it all, I now had renewed hope that perhaps he was also there to help me with my personal battles.

Until this time, I had not actually prayed. I did not want to appear foolish even to myself by talking to a being that either was not there or did not have the capacity to hear and respond to me. But now, with my new insight into the nature of God as revealed by Jesus, I felt I could talk to Him because I could talk to Jesus, who was both God and man.

For the first time, on that bus, I prayed. I did not recite any formal prayers like the Our Father, which I knew by now. I spoke to God directly, telling him of all that was in my heart, the life I was dissatisfied with; asking him to help me to be better. There was no parting of the clouds or a loud voice responding to my words. I sat in silence with God, at peace, confident that I had been heard and that I was no longer going to struggle alone.

Over the next couple of days, I told Bruce and Dr. Campbell about my acceptance of Jesus as God's son. The first thing I wanted to do, since Jesus said that it was necessary in order to enter heaven, was to be baptized. However, I soon discovered that getting baptized was not as simple as I anticipated. I had to pick a church to be baptized into and in order to do this I had to learn about the particular teachings of each church. This became a daunting task when I learned that beside the Roman Catholic Church and the Brethren there were dozens of protestant sects, each claiming to be the true church Jesus wanted established on earth. How was I to choose and how long would it all take? I wanted to be a full Christian and felt a great urgency about my baptism.

Of course, there was Dr. Campbell, very much promoting the virtues of the Catholic Church. Bruce, while no longer a follower of the Brethren, had many objections to and questions about the Catholic Church, which had been ingrained in him since he was a child. While I listened to their arguments, I wanted to make up my own mind.

At this time, Bruce, who under the influence of Dr. Campbell had become more and more interested in Aristotelian and Thomistic philosophy, heard from the University of Laval in Quebec City, that he had been accepted into the Masters Philosophy program. Within a couple of weeks, at the end of August, he would be moving to Quebec. By now, our relationship had strengthened, and since my acceptance of God and Jesus as his Son, most of our disagreements vanished. We did not want to be separated for months and so I decided to put my studies on hold and go with Bruce to Quebec.

I found an apartment on Rue St. Louis inside the walls of the old city, and Bruce took up an apartment with a fellow student on Rue St. Jean outside the walls. Without realizing it at the time, the changes in my life brought about by this move, became a significant influence in my conversion journey. At first, I missed Dr. Campbell and all my old friends and activities. Dr. Campbell had instructed us to seek out Dr. Warren Murray, a friend of his, who was a professor of Thomistic philosophy at Laval. Though all the classes at Laval were taught in French, Dr. Murray was an Anglophone and gave a couple of classes in English to a small group of English speaking students. Bruce and I joined this group and soon they became our new circle of friends. All of these students were Catholic and most had previously studied at Thomas Aquinas College in California. Their actively lived faith, their lifestyle, their dedication to seeking truth, was a sharp contrast to the life and milieu Bruce and I had left behind in Waterloo. They gave a great example of what day to day dedicated Catholic life was like among people our own age. I found their self-confidence, their joyful generosity, and their obvious personal relationship with God, very attractive.

Towards the end of October Bruce and I became engaged. Anxious to be married as soon as possible, we set our wedding date for Jan.2, the end of the Christmas school break. Though we wanted a very simple and small wedding with just our immediate families, when I called my parents in Toronto to discuss the plans with them, it was clear that they had something more elaborate in mind. Since Bruce and I were in no position to pay for our wedding, I agreed to let my parents organize everything, promising that we would turn up for the event.

I had not yet given any hint to them about my conversion to Christianity. I didn't think it was necessary to burden them with something they would find very upsetting. They knew Bruce was a Christian, but, because they liked him so much, they did not raise any objections to a mixed marriage, as long as the ceremony would be Jewish. It did mean though, that they had to find a special Rabbi who could officiate over mixed marriages.

According to plan, we were married on Jan. 2, 1977. I arrived in Toronto two weeks before to pick out a wedding dress, (a rental), and to meet with the Rabbi who was to officiate over the ceremony. While I was not a sentimental person and didn't like ceremonies or rituals, I did want to make sure that our wedding included the essential Christian elements; that we were married before God and for life. The Rabbi, who was used to mixed marriage ceremonies, readily agreed to include whatever words and phrases I wanted into both what he said, and into our vows. Two days after the wedding, we returned to Quebec city and began our married life in my small one room apartment.

With Bruce, who was now also very interested in discovering which church was the one that most closely followed the teachings of Jesus, we started to attend the various English speaking (and some

50

French) churches around the city. We lived just inside the walls of Old Quebec and there were several churches of different denominations within walking distance. At the Protestant churches, we tried to connect with people with whom we could talk about their particular beliefs. We continued to learn about Catholicism from our friends, Warren Murray, and some priests to whom they introduced us.

Several differences between the Protestant and Catholic Church soon became apparent and I found it confusing to try to muddle my way through understanding which was right. Yet, there were three points that distinctly stood out in my mind:

1. **The Catholic Church** was the only one with a central teaching authority. While I didn't yet accept the infallibility of the Pope, it made a lot of sense that Jesus would ensure that God's will was clearly made known throughout time. I liked the idea of an infallible Pope.

2. **The Catholic Church** was the only one that insisted on the necessity of confession – confession to a priest. I felt the need to go to confession and to actually hear that my sins were forgiven. I liked the idea that with confession I would receive a special grace from God to help me in my personal battles. In addition, I recognized that with time, it was inevitable that my faith would waver in its intensity. I sensed that the sacrament of confession would help to keep me on track and keep me from straying.

**3. The Catholic Church** was the only one that truly believed in the presence of Jesus in the Eucharist. From my reading of the gospels, especially the gospel of St. John, it was very clear to me that this is exactly what Jesus meant. He even said that this would be 'a stumbling block' for many. Yet it was clear to me, that he meant this to be taken seriously. When Jesus passed the bread and wine around at the last supper, he re-emphasized that his followers were to eat and drink his body and blood in the guise of bread and wine.

It was primarily on the basis of this one point that, even though I still didn't understand many things about the Catholic Church, I chose it as the church into which I would be baptised. If the Church was so right on this one fundamental point, which no other church supported, I reasoned, than I could trust it to be right about other things too. I wanted to be baptised as soon as possible and I was willing for now, to accept most of the other teachings on faith.

I asked Père Lacasse, a Jesuit priest whom I had come to know, to prepare me for baptism and I began seeing him for instruction about once a week. While Bruce completely supported my entry into the Catholic Church, he was not yet prepared to make a similar decision. He still had too many theological questions about Church doctrine that he needed answered, – questions that I also had, but which for me were secondary to my desire for baptism. Practically and morally, we accepted and valued the teachings of the Church.

Père Lacasse suggested that we set the day for my baptism for January 28, the feast day of St. Thomas Aquinas. This seemed very appropriate since my introduction to St. Thomas's teachings was foundational to my understanding of Christianity and the Catholic Church.

By that time, we had moved to a slightly larger apartment in the old city, just a five-minute walk from the Basilique Notre Dame de Quebec. The Basilica had several daily masses and I had gotten into the habit of stopping in there when I passed, either to attend mass or just to pray.

It was at the Basilica, in a private ceremony, that my baptism took place on the afternoon of Jan.28. I had asked Dr. Campbell and his wife Martha to be my godparents. Since they could not attend in person, two of our friends stood in for them. There were only a few others present. I did not know what was customary procedure around a baptism and so I did not plan a big celebration. My main concern was being baptised. I wanted to do what Jesus commanded and I could hardly wait to start anew, free from the sins and guilt of the past. I wanted to be able to truly call God my father and to have the support of the sacraments and the church in my life.

After the baptism, Bruce and I walked to St. Peter's Church, outside the old city walls, to attend a late afternoon Mass at St. Peter's, an Anglophone parish. I wanted to be able to understand every word of the Mass at which I was to receive my first communion. Also, later that evening we were going to attend another mass at the Dominican Church with all our friends followed by a big feast in honour of St. Thomas. I didn't want to receive my first communion in front of all the people I knew with the distraction of what they might be thinking or expecting of me. I wanted to focus my attention on Jesus with whom I would be intimately united for the first time. I don't remember the particular details of my thoughts and feelings as I received communion, except that I was at peace. I had done what Jesus commanded. He was with me, ready to help me start a new Christian life. The "power" that I always knew was out there and that I always felt loved me wasn't some vague power at all. It was a person, and it was Jesus.

Baptism began the second stage of my conversion as I now set about learning how to live a Catholic life. I got a boost two years later when my husband Bruce was also baptized and confirmed into the Catholic Church. We began to travel the journey together.

Over the next several years, with the loving guidance of outstanding Catholic friends, we became familiar with Catholic traditions and customs. I learned to celebrate the major feasts of the liturgical year and to raise our growing family with a knowledge and love for God. (Our first son was born a year and a half after we were married and our second son a year after that with four more children to follow over the next decade.) In challenging circumstances, I learned to trust the ageless wisdom of the Church. Living with my husband and our two young children on a teaching assistant's income, we followed the Church's teachings on contraception.

54

At the same time, wanting to discover the reasons behind it, we read Humanae Vitae. That document made so much sense that after finishing it, I was prouder than ever to be a Catholic and grateful that God had led me to the Church. Doing God's will was difficult sometimes, but I learned that it was also a great adventure and ultimately good.

I also began daily, meditative prayer. I read 'Introduction to the Devout Life' by St. Francis de Sales, 'Divine Intimacy' by Fr. Gabriel of St. Mary Magdalen, and 'The Practice of Christian Perfection' by St. Rodriguez. The more I read and learned, the more I longed for a spiritual director such as the one St. Francis talked about: someone I could trust to guide me in the circumstances of my life to the goals that God had for me. With the increasing challenges of raising our children and running the household, I frequently felt that the peace and serenity of holiness was far removed from my practical everyday life.

Then, through a friend who attended a weekly discussion group that we hosted at our house, we learned about Opus Dei. Opus Dei, we discovered, was an organization in the Catholic Church founded by St. Josemaria Escriva, dedicated to helping individuals turn every aspect of their daily lives into opportunities of growing closer to God. It offered personal spiritual direction as well as doctrinal formation. For me, it provided the dedicated, traditional guidance in leading a Christian life that I had been anticipating since I joined the Catholic Church. Through the formation I received, I felt that I was making headway in recognizing God's presence in all the circumstances of my life. This support helped me to face a major challenge about ten years after my baptism.

When I was baptized, Père Lacasse had advised me that for the time being, I say nothing to my parents about my conversion because it would make them very upset. The shaky relationship we had since my arrival in Canada, had improved once I married Bruce. I was reluctant to do anything to destroy the progress we had made. Since we lived far apart and only saw each other a few times a year, we managed to keep my conversion hidden. Any Christian customs we kept, they always attributed to Bruce, especially since they made no distinction between Catholics and other Christians.

Then one year my parents invited us to spend a long weekend at their cottage. From, there, getting to the nearest town to attend Sunday Mass, would take considerable effort and use a sizable chunk of the time we had for visiting with my parents. I thought it better to give them advance notice. On previous occasions when we visited in the city, I had said that I wanted to accompany Bruce to church, and they happily watched the children while we were gone. But now, our oldest boys were also able to receive communion and we wanted to go as a family. When I called to tell my Dad, he became angry that Bruce would force his whole family to go to church with him, and cut into the time we had to spend together. I realized that it was time to tell my Dad about my conversion. When I told him that it was not Bruce forcing me, but that I was going with him because I had converted, my Dad hung up the phone. We never went to the cottage that summer. In fact, my Dad did not speak with us for two years, not even to the children. I spoke with my Mom every couple of weeks, but she always ended up in tears.

Then, I became pregnant with our sixth child and my Mom could not stay away once the baby was born. She came and we spent a wonderful week together. She was very impressed with how our family was progressing, especially how well behaved the children were and how well they got along together. She acknowledged the positive influence that our faith had in the way we raised our children, in the way Bruce and I interacted and in the way we behaved with others. When she returned home, she convinced my Dad to relent and to come and visit. They came a few months later and amidst the enthusiastic reception they received from their grandchildren, we were reconciled.

One year, my parents decided to visit over the Easter weekend. That year, the Jewish Passover coincided perfectly with Holy Thursday. Not knowing this, my mother suggested that they come in time to celebrate the Passover with us. At first, I was in a quandary, not wanting to confuse our children with two different religious celebrations. But then, I remembered hearing about a book called *Christ in the Passover*, written by a Jewish convert, that explains the Passover in light of Christianity. I purchased the book and used it to help me plan the Passover celebration. Again, I prepared my parents by explaining that I wanted our children to understand the Passover and how it related to our faith and customs. I explained that we would include some of our explanations with the Seder ritual. They accepted this readily.

The celebration, which we anticipated with some fear and trembling, was very successful. As my father recited the prayers, performed the traditional rituals and passed around the food items from the Seder plate, Bruce and I explained how this related to the actions and words of Jesus at the time of the last supper, as well as to what the priest did during Mass. It was a great learning experience for all of us and my mother commented that she was impressed by our knowledge of the Jewish faith and customs. Juxtaposing the two celebrations, it became clear that God foreknew Jesus' passion, death, and resurrection back at the time of the Exodus. It saddened me that my parents didn't see the obvious -that Jesus was the Messiah – that all of Jewish history foretold his mission.

After that, my parents grew increasingly more accepting of our Catholic faith to the point of occasionally accompanying us to Mass when they come to visit. When one of our sons entered the Seminary in 2008, they were complacent and accepting.

Thirty years have passed since my baptism. In many respects my conversion is still unfolding as daily I continue to discover new truths contained within the richness of Church doctrine and learn to turn my heart ever closer to God. In all this, I am ever confident of the presence of His love, which has guided me throughout my life.

# Douglas Farrow

Douglas Farrow is Professor of Christian Thought at McGill University. He is the author of Ascension and Ecclesia, Recognizing Religion in a Secular Society, Nation of Bastards, and other books. He and his wife, Anna, reside in Baie d'Urfé with their five children.

## "Are You Catholic?"

When I arrived for the first time, weary from a long night's flight and more than a little bedraggled, at the door I was seeking in King's College, on the Strand, I was wearing a large wooden cross, crafted by a friend. As it happened, I was met not only by the eminent professor who was to become my Doktorvater, but also by an equally eminent scholar and churchman, who some three years earlier had been made Metropolitan of Pergamon. Standing next to Colin Gunton was the Most Reverend John Zizioulas, who seemed to me (the titular nature of his appointment notwithstanding) an exotic figure connected to the mysterious world of the Apocalypse. Espying the cross, he enquired, "Are you Catholic?" "No," I replied, "I'm an Anglican."

That was more than twenty years ago and the answer has changed. Being a theologian (one much indebted to the two far better theologians already introduced) my account of the change will be

59

theological as well as autobiographical. The short-comings in both dimensions I beg the reader to forgive. This mixed genre is not one in which I have had much practice, and lapses of memory or judgment, perhaps also of gratitude or charity, are sure to take their toll. The task, in any case, is a difficult one: to give an account of oneself that is not unintelligible either to friends and acquaintances or to complete strangers, while speaking of that which far transcends oneself, since it touches on what Zizioulas calls the ecclesial hypostasis and hence on the church itself. Indulgences will be required, and I assume that one who reads such a book will not be sparing of indulgences, even for the sometimes self-indulgent.

*

In 1988, when I disembarked from the plane that had carried me to London, I was bedraggled inwardly as well as outwardly. Truth be told, I was emotionally exhausted and hardly ready to begin a new life in a city I had never even visited. In London, the infused corpuscles of myriad peoples pulse through ancient Anglo-Saxon arteries, mixing in unpredictable ways with the now dwindling native supply. In London, one might very well meet a quick-witted English dissenter, with a working-class background but an Oxford education, standing side-by-side with a grave and thoughtful and rather shy Greek archbishop, ambassador of the Ecumenical Patriarch, talking theology. But the cross around my neck was a tangible link to the tightly knit circle of fellowship from which I had only the day before been prised. There, in that British Columbian valley, where I was born, the only ancient arteries are clefts in the rugged hills. And, of course, Lake Okanagan, which winds some ninety miles north to south, filling that dry countryside with water and tinting its hills with the delicate but invigorating light that reflects from its surface. In its depths, the serpent-like Ogopogo, the lake demon called by the natives *n'ha-a-itk*, is still said to swim.

A far more ancient and less benign serpent had found its way into the Anglican Diocese of Kootenay, or so it appeared to those of us who for the past two years had been engaged in an agonizing struggle for the soul of that diocese, itself barely a century old. I cannot say very much about the form in which it came, except that its effects were common enough: a failure of integrity in the highest places; clergy corrupted by scandal and fear; laity divided and adrift; dwindling numbers in the pews, the registers, and the financial ledgers. A spark of revival glowed in the heat on the west side of the lake, threatening a gospel brush fire, but it was quickly dashed by buckets of water hurled at it by seasoned diocesan hands. In a kitchen in Kelowna a retired Canadian primate sat with us, acting as ambassador for his successor in far-off Toronto, brokering a peace that, if not exactly a godly peace, would at least avert the kind of peace that only lawyers can bring. There was an exorcism of sorts, but healing and restoration there was not, prayer and fasting and self-examination notwithstanding. For the Diocese of Kootenay was but a local widening in a river of faith that had crossed the country, east to west, in the days of the British pioneers, but flowed now, theologically speaking, to a foreign sea. That was not entirely obvious to me at the time, however, for reasons that may become clearer if I tell a bit more of my story.

I was raised in a Protestant home, of mixed English and Scottish stock.[2] On both sides the family had for some time been Baptist by persuasion. I asked for baptism at age eight, after we moved to Cranbrook from Summerland, and was immersed in the waters under the dais of the First Baptist Church in that town. Much later, after college and seminary training in evangelical institutions in Manitoba and Indiana, respectively, I briefly considered ordination to ministry in the Christian and Missionary Alliance. Having received a call to become an associate at a prominent Vancouver church, I withdrew by motorcycle into the mountains of Montana to reflect.

It had been a curious experience. When I sat for my interview among the twenty-four elders, the first question was, "Why do you wear a beard?" I explained that I was actually a Hutterite, which at least satisfied them that seminary (a seminary of the Grace Brethren, not the Hutterite Brethren) hadn't destroyed my sense of humour. From there the elders and I got on fine, though the senior pastor made clear afterwards that the beard would have to go. I suppose his ecumenical instincts didn't extend as

---

[2] On my mother's side I am part Matheson, from Skye, and part Nelson; this is probably sufficient to account for my peculiarities. On my father's side, the family hails from Norfolk and Suffolk, coming to Canada from London in the 19th C. The obituary of my great, great grandmother, Sara Jane Farrow, claims that she was the first white woman in the Bruce Peninsula.

far as Hutterites. Anyway, as I lay under a full moon on the mountainside, high in grizzly country – starting, I confess, throughout the night at every low grunt or snuffle of friendlier beasts – I knew that that was not the place for me. I don't mean Vancouver, that glistening gem set between mountains and sea, for Vancouver is exactly where I went. But I went to Regent College to resume my theological studies, and to prepare myself for the doctoral work that would take me eventually to London.

It was at Regent that I encountered the renowned evangelical Anglican, J. I. Packer, who supervised my work on Oscar Cullmann. There also that I studied with visiting professors Anthony Thiselton, N. T. Wright, and J. B. Torrance, and spent a very lively week in the company of T. F. Torrance. At Regent, lectures and readings in theology, philosophy, literature, hermeneutics and history opened me to a much wider world of scholarship, and to a wider conception of Christianity. It also prepared me, if somewhat haphazardly, for what I afterwards found at the parish of St. George's, Westbank, pastored then by the Reverend John Briscall – namely, a parish life ordered and nourished by the Eucharistic liturgy and alive with the joy of the Holy Spirit. St. George's was where that spark was glowing and the gospel brush fire threatening to break out.

My evangelical Protestant upbringing had been very rich in its way. It was full of scripture and song, evangelism and missions, fellowship and prayer. If there was an element of sectarian presumption (even Regent was not free of that) and some earnest silliness too, there was more fundamentally the humility and sobriety that come from taking seriously the urging of St. Peter that Christians should regard themselves as "aliens and exiles," as members of a religious diaspora that must last until the parousia. There was also, of course, a certain anti-Catholic instinct – not, in this case, of the ethnic or cultural variety but of the theological. Catholics believed in salvation by works and thus sinned against grace; they practiced superstitious rituals and discouraged personal interest in the scriptures; in short, they were in need of conversion. Even baptism they obviously did not understand, since they baptized babies, as if to inoculate them against any eventual conversion.

During the second war, when my father was stationed in the Gaspé, my mother gave birth to my eldest sibling. Helen was not only Bryce and Kay's first baby; she was the first Protestant baby (if an unbaptised baby can be Protestant) to be born in that region. The hospital nuns were very kind, but since she was not to be baptized, they did not know how to register her birth. Having made enquiry with the central authorities, they were instructed to open a new record book just for her. My parents, I believe, were impressed with the treatment they received. Not long after, mind you, my mother's brother, an enthusiastic Baptist of a Calvinist persuasion, having returned wounded from Italy, decided to do some itinerate preaching in Québec. (Even bullets couldn't put holes in the spirit of the irrepressible Reverend Lorne Matheson!) He was arrested and briefly imprisoned for his troubles, reinforcing the notion in our family that Catholic cultures were not after all entirely accommodating of Protestants.[3]

My own experience with Catholicism began inauspiciously. Though a layman, I had been invited to serve as secretary to the Cranbrook Ministerial Association in view of an ecumenical educational enterprise I was leading.[4] I soon found myself in the sitting room of one of the local Catholic pastors: a very talented priest, with a thriving parish; a musical man who was also a school principal. No doubt I told him that I had visited a few Catholic schools in the mid-seventies, when I was working on the prairies with the "gospel rock" band, Brotherlove. Fr. Buckley tested me by showing me some Chick tracts, imported from California, that an anti-Catholic zealot had been handing out in the parish. (Folk who aren't familiar with Chick Publications have been leading a sheltered life, and may not know, for example, about Alberto Rivera's claims that the Catholic Church created Islam and conspired to bring about the Russian Revolution, the Holocaust, etc. Rivera was featured in several of Jack Chick's comic books.) Naturally this scandalized Fr. Buckley. But his parish,

---

[3] The Jehovah's Witnesses, of course, had already put the Catholic authorities on edge.

[4] To my partners in that enterprise I dedicated my first book, *The Word of Truth and Disputes about Words*, on which I was working at the time, while also trying to write my thesis on Cullmann. The over-heavy use of capitalization in that book betrays the spell cast on me by T. F. Torrance.

unfortunately, and the whole region, would shortly be scandalized in an incomparably deeper way, when in 1989 he was convicted and jailed for a multitude of sexual abuse offences.

Just as one does not judge Protestantism by the rabid anti-Catholicism of Jack Chick[5], however, or Catholicism by the virulent anti-Semitism one finds on the web pages of Christusrex, one should not judge either by the sexual abuse crisis that is still unfolding, which is by no means confined to Christian contexts. One should indeed be scandalized, horrified, and driven to one's knees in prayer. Yet one should not be entirely surprised. For truth attracts lies, and stumbling blocks must come. Moreover there is today, on a multitude of fronts, and behind the lines in the church itself, an assault on everything that witnesses, or ought to witness, to "the Father from whom every family in heaven and on earth is named."

At the time I didn't know much about the sexual abuse crisis, of course, and remarkably little about the Catholic Church. I was suspicious of sectarianism, however, about which I knew rather more, and at Regent I had learned to be interested in the sacraments. Curiously, it took a visiting Scottish Presbyterian professor to pique my interest. James Torrance (whose son, Alan, would later become a colleague and close friend when I taught at King's)

---

[5] I haven't followed Jack Chick's career, but I wonder whether he is working these days with the folk who produce manuals for Québec's new *Ethics and Religious Culture* programme, some of which offer anti-Catholic comics and cartoons that remind me of nothing more than a Chick tract!

was lecturing at Regent in the summer of 1984 and I was his teaching assistant. He had studied with Cullmann, on whose christology I was working, and had translated Early Christian Worship into English. His passion for a theology nurtured by and for authentic Christian worship was palpable. So was his passion for a theology that could nurture human community, in the city of man as well as the city of God, without being commandeered by the devil (as had Dutch Calvinism in South Africa, for example).

After one of Professor Torrance's lectures on the sacraments, in which he had criticized the notion that baptism and the Eucharist were merely responses to grace – expressions and "badges" of our faith – rather than acts of grace, I had my first catholic moment, so to say, without yet understanding what was happening. That is, I had my first inkling that a firm belief in the priority of grace did not entail the sacramental nominalism on which I had been raised, but rather repudiated it.[6] So dumbfounded was I by the thought that God, rather than man, might after all be the primary agent in the sacraments, that I put the question directly to Professor Torrance the next time I saw him. The question, as I recall, was rather crudely framed: "Do you mean to say that God himself actually does something in the consecration of the bread and wine?" To my surprise, he did not answer me. He said nothing at all, perhaps thinking me rather duller than he had hoped

---

[6] By this expression I do not mean a nominalist account of transubstantiation, for example, but any approach that denies an objective (extra-mental) relation between the sign and the thing signified.

– or, just possibly, realizing that he had started something best left to another Teacher.

*

In the autumn of that year John Paul II came to Canada as Vicar of Christ (a title I still assumed, in good Protestant fashion, to designate an office that did not exist, though I wanted no part with the placard-carrying Paisley types). Back in Cranbrook, I watched and listened as he preached on television from the Big O in Montreal, and thought to myself that I had not heard, in a very long while, a sermon as centred on Christ as the one he preached to the youth who were gathered there. "I wish to speak to you about the light of Christ, because it is as a witness of the Redeemer that I have come before you..." (Most Protestant sermons, whether liberal or conservative, are about you and me, or someone the preacher mistakes for you or me, rather than about Jesus; unfortunately this can be said of most Catholic sermons too.) At the time I had no idea that twenty-one years on I would be sitting in front of a television set in Montreal, watching the vigil in St. Peter's Square during John Paul II's final moments, as a newly-confirmed Catholic who felt himself deeply indebted to the man. I was not yet an Anglican, though I soon would be.

I had begun reading Karl Barth at seminary, and was now taking Barth in large doses. At the same time, however, I was moving in the direction of the Torrance brothers on the sacraments, which was the opposite direction from that of Barth himself. T. F. Torrance, who headed the team responsible for the English translation of the Church Dogmatics, had discouraged Barth from publishing the last fragments thereof, which reveal his Zwinglian and indeed his Baptistic drift, placing even baptism under the rubric of ethics – something we do in response to the gospel, rather than something God does in effecting the gospel. I had begun asking my Baptist brethren – aspiring theologians have bad habits like this – how it was that they called themselves Baptists. If baptism doesn't save, but merely attests to salvation, why make such a big deal of it? If so many heroes of the faith, even Protestant heroes like Luther and Calvin, were never really baptized, having received only the rite of infant baptism (which was no baptism at all), what need had a Christian of baptism? It might be a good thing but hardly a necessary thing.

The ecclesiological implications were not yet fully obvious to me, but I began to intuit something, at least, of the relation between sacramental grace and holy orders: that the latter belongs to the former and that order in the church, being itself a form of grace, does not ascend from below except that it first descend from above. But this in turn raised the question of history; that is, of the relation between the institutional character of the church (its longitude, if you please) and its pneumatological and Eucharistic constitution in the present (its latitude). The church needed to be located theologically on this grid, as Zizioulas argued in Being as Communion. If the Roman church tended to neglect latitude, as Zizioulas thought, its Protestant offshoots had trouble even with longitude.

About this time I returned to the Okanagan to teach at a small evangelical bible college.[7] My first assignments were in church history and the history of western civilization. I found it necessary to inform my students that the great gap theory, as I called it, would not be the operative assumption. The church had not come into existence with the apostles, faded with the fathers, and been restored in the Reformation (whether the 'magisterial' or the 'radical' Reformation). The problem of history would have to be taken much more seriously than that, and so would the problem of ontology – the problem of the being and nature of the church.

What was at first a theoretical issue became an experiential one when I encountered the presence of God in the weekly Eucharistic celebrations at St. George's, which I had occasion to visit. This experience was quite unexpected and profoundly moving, as even non-Christian visitors sometimes attested. It brought home to me the difference between the non-sacramental worship[8] to which I was accustomed and the richness of the tradition. Not only was the latter's liturgy of the word thicker and more substantial, feeding the mind on the old covenant and the new, its Eucharistic rite held out the

---

[7] The Okanagan Bible College, at which I taught from 1986-1988, no longer exists, but I take no responsibility for that.

[8] I do not say non-liturgical, for even as a child I had noticed how church meetings of every stripe had predictable forms and patterns of language. I used to count the number of times my first pastor in the Christian and Missionary Alliance would say "this morning hour," for example; if memory serves he managed a total in the twenties on one occasion.

Bread of Life even to one's hands and one's lips, while the Spirit united the one body under one head.

There were other places in Kelowna where the Spirit, which blows where it wills, was evidently at work, as I knew from my students, some of whom were having experiences commonly called charismatic. Experiences vary, of course, and must be interpreted, just as prophecy must be tested. It seemed to me that Anglicanism offered a framework for interpretation that was at once attentive to what the Spirit had taught the church over the centuries (longitude again) and open to what the Spirit might teach the church here and now (latitude again). I was not certain how to interpret some of the charismatic phenomena that presented themselves inside and outside of Anglican circles; nor was I certain about many points of ecclesiology or sacramental theology, for example. But the problem of unity was pressing itself upon me more than the problem of certainty. The Spirit may blow where and as it wills, but it remains the Spirit of unity; the breath of God does not blow apart the churches or the brethren. It was the problem of unity, not of certainty, that pushed me to consider making, not merely the parish of St. George's, but the Diocese of Kootenay – though I knew it to be in a very sorry state – my ecclesial home; that is, to ask for the sacrament of confirmation and to be received into the Anglican communion. At that time I believed the Anglican communion not only to have adopted a via media in its liturgy, doctrine, and discipline, but to represent a via media ecumenically: to be a bridge between Catholicism and Protestantism and, as such, an avenue and impetus to unity, the unity of the Spirit.[9]

I was confirmed and received in the midst of the tempest that was rising in the territorially vast teapot that was Kootenay. When that tempest had nearly abated, though its wreckage was still being strewn on both sides of the valley, I departed for England to take up my scholarship at King's. I arrived a few weeks later than I'd hoped and in the spent state already described. A fellow student who lived in Islington – a good-hearted Glaswegian to whom Professor Gunton had introduced me – took me in. A couple of days later I went up to Oxford to visit the Wright family. Their familiar faces notwithstanding, I felt rather lost and bewildered, like Paul and friends must have felt that first night on Malta. I found myself out in a dark meadow, warming myself with mulled wine, as near as I could stand to the blazing fire. It was Guy Fawkes Night.

*

Settling in at King's, I commenced my thesis research under Colin Gunton, to whom Tony Thiselton had directed me when I began making enquiries about doctoral work. Colin, who died the year The Da Vinci Code was published, would have been amused to discover that the solution to the protagonist's puzzle was worked out in the King's College Research Institute in Systematic Theology, which Dan Brown apparently thought esoteric enough to incorporate into his best-seller (though in one of

---

[9] I was blissfully ignorant of Newman's invention and subsequent repudiation of this myth.

his lesser liberties with history he lodged it in much swankier Westminster quarters than King's could provide). Colin was the founder and the heart and soul of the Institute. That was the place to do systematic theology in those days, at least in Britain, if you believed that theology was just as vital to the twentieth century as to the fourth, and that it could still build on what had been achieved in the fourth. At the Society for the Study of Theology, which Colin had helped to revitalize, certain wags took to referring to students of his (among them myself and my Scottish friend, Graham McFarlane) as Gunton's Gurkhas. We were all deep into Barth, of course, who had done more than anyone else to shake Protestant theology from its slumbers – Catholic theology, too, owed him a great debt, as the Vatican itself recognized – but we were deep into many other sources of inspiration as well. For me it was St. Irenaeus, in whom I found, at the very roots of church dogmatics, a treasure trove of theological insight and a theological mind that was catholic before anyone quite knew what it meant to be catholic.[10]

I was tutoring undergraduates in Barth, however, not in Irenaeus, when providentially

---

[10] "The church, having received this preaching and this faith, although scattered throughout the world, yet, as if occupying but one house, carefully preserves it" (*Against heresies* 1.10.2). It not only preserves it, however, but as Irenaeus's own work makes clear, it brings forth from it treasures both new and old. The discovery of Irenaeus was an important turning point for me, as anyone who reads the third chapter of *Ascension and Ecclesia* might guess.

something appeared from under the Californian sun, via Woldingham in Surrey – a Catholic boarding school for girls – that would change my life. Anna Susan Domini Whelan turned out to be the "one quite bright American" whom Colin had indicated would complete the seminar group, and before too long we were discussing things other than Barth. Our first date, as I recall, was for an Advent carol service at Southwark Cathedral. A couple of years later, after she had returned to the States and I to Canada to continue writing up my thesis, we became engaged. We were married in the summer of 1992 at St. Rita's, a retreat centre near Gold Hill in Oregon, run at the time by her uncle, Fr. Tom Whelan, an Augustinian priest. Fr. William Springer, a priest from San Diego de Alcala, the mission that prides itself on being "the birthplace of Christianity in the far West," prepared us for that event and gave the homily, entitled *Mi casa es su casa*. Though I was not yet a Catholic – my own pastor from St. George's, the Reverend John Briscall, assisted at the liturgy – I received communion at the Mass within which our marriage took place. In the far West certain provisions of the Second Vatican Council for separated brethren who find themselves in remote places have sometimes been generously interpreted.

## *Mi Casa Es Su Casa*

At that time inter-marriage between Anglicans and Catholics was regarded, with ecumenical optimism, as creating a bridge between the two communions in the form of the domestic church.

DOUGLAS FARROW

That is certainly how we saw it ourselves. Such
bridges were not without their obstacles, of course,
but my parents-in-law (very devout Catholics) were
not among them. Vincent, who served as legal advisor to the bishop of San Diego, welcomed me both
as a son-in-law and as a young theologian with
"traditional" instincts, and took a lively interest in
my work, as did Barbara. This was of great encouragement to me. Even vigorous debate with a family
friend, Fr. Vincent Martin, at St. Andrew's Abbey
in Valyermo – where I appeared perhaps a little too
traditional for Fr. Vincent, whose years at the Tan-
tur Ecumenical Institute and whose work in Jewish-
Christian dialogue had led him to search for ways of
understanding Jesus and the Church with which I
could not entirely agree – did not dampen my father-in-law's enthusiasm for my work or for that of
those who had influenced me, including Colin Gunton and Tom Wright.

Anna and I spent the first two years of our marriage at Regent College, where I taught a rather controversial course in ecclesiology and eschatology
that took the Eucharist as its systematic centre, and
continued work on my dissertation. She did an M.A.
degree with a thesis (under Eugene Peterson's direction) on the Holy Saturday motif in the spirituality of Hans Urs von Balthasar. Then in 1994 we
returned to England after I was offered a lectureship
in theology back at King's College.

Those years were mainly Anglican years,
though we had some Catholic friends. We lived at
first in a rectory in Sutton during an interregnum at
the parish of St. Nicholas, which I served as a lay

reader. (The priest in charge, and the rector eventually appointed, were both faithful women.) Two children were born to us there, after we moved to a nearby flat, and both were baptized in an Anglican context. At one point we contemplated moving away from the city, and drove far into the countryside to look at the family home of a Catholic priest who wished it to have lodgers. The place had a "priest hole," and the family memory of persecution was evident still in the priest himself, though he and it seemed all very foreign to me.

By now I knew rather more about the world of Anglicanism, however – or at least about Anglicanism in the Anglosphere – and doubts about its direction were beginning to grow. My interest in Orthodoxy and in Catholicism was growing too, but I was yet a long way from serious thoughts of converting. As for England, we had a mind to remain there permanently, it and the rest of the British Isles being much to our liking. But with both our families in North America, and my post not yet being permanent, we occasionally entertained thoughts of crossing the Atlantic again. In the autumn of 1997 a post in theology came open at McGill and I put in for it. When I was offered it, we made hasty preparations for departure. I sometimes fancy that we were just in time. In Blair's Britain what Guy Fawkes had witnessed only in his dreams, before he leapt from the gallows, was actually taking place: the slow-motion destruction of Westminster and everything it once stood for. That Tony Blair, in recent days and for his own reasons, also became a Catholic, I think of as a grand irony.[11]

\*

Landing in Montreal on the eve of the great ice storm of January 1998, I noticed the odd fluctuations of temperature as the plane descended. Soon the transmission towers were buckling and the tree branches crashing down. My first lectures at McGill were written by candlelight, without benefit of electricity. But I was glad to be back in Canada, and in the most European corner of Canada, where traces of Paris, London, Glasgow and Edinburgh could be found side by side on the city streets.

This part of the country was new to me, however; neither Anna nor I had set foot in Montreal before. We were immediately befriended by a fine Anglican priest from St. George's, Place du Canada, the Reverend Brett Cane. I took up my post at McGill as a parishioner of St. George's, which we continued to attend after moving to Baie d'Urfé in the West Island. Among members of the Faculty of Religious Studies, Anglicanism was the best represented form of Christianity or any other religion. But I was now, for the first time, in territory that was Catholic both historically and culturally. It would be some time before I would have occasion to read Leo XIII's *Affari vos* (the only papal encyclical to be addressed specifically to Canadians) but I had come to a land to which it could indeed be said that "the love of the Catholic Church

---

[11] Fawkes was himself a convert, of course.

stood by the cradle of your State"[12] – a fact not wholly forgotten in Québec, even by those who wish to forget it.

Gradually I began to make Catholic friends (Professor David Williams and Dr Daniel Cere among them) and to attend more Catholic liturgies, but only gradually. At the same time, my work on the doctrine of the ascension had begun to turn my attention to church-state issues and to questions about the nature of political authority. In the first year of the new millennium I began planning a conference in Pluralism, Religion and Public Policy, the execution of which engaged me more heavily with Catholic (as well as Orthodox and Jewish) friends and colleagues.[13] The conference, held in October 2002, grew out of a Faculty discussion about possible guest lecturers from which the name of Fr. Richard John Neuhaus emerged. I volunteered to contact him and things took off from there. Fr. Richard came, and his Beatty lecture was one of several conference highlights. It was not uncontroversial, of course, but the confident treatment of his topic, "Liberal Democracy and Acts of Faith," in his rich baritone voice and measured cadences, seemed to elicit from the heavily Catholic audience that evening a palpable sense of relief that it was possible to speak confidently in the public square as a

---

[12] *Affari vos* (On the Manitoba School Question, 1897) §1. Leo had Québec especially in mind, and the civilizing work of Bishop Laval in particular.

[13] Among new Catholic friends was Iain Benson, founding director of the Centre for Cultural Renewal, who became a partner in the arrangements.

Catholic. Claude Ryan, who gave a thoughtful address in the opening session of the conference – one of his last public appearances – also made an impression.

If I continued to draw on Anglican resources intellectually (including in particular the work of Oliver O'Donovan) it was increasingly in Catholic circles that I now discovered interesting examples of a publicly engaged Christianity. My collaboration and friendship with Daniel Cere, who at the time was still director of the Newman Centre, was developing. His patient and generous spirit, his intellectual curiosity and measured judgments, combined with the personal influence of Anna and her family to give me a deepening sense of the possibility of being Catholic. That was not something I was directly contemplating as yet, but another door was about to open. At dinner one evening during the conference, Fr. Richard, who had just penned a very positive review of Ascension and Ecclesia for the next issue of First Things, remarked that I'd been rather hard on the mediaeval church and on its mariology in particular. I replied that I hoped some day to offer a more constructive treatment of mariology.[14] Not long afterwards he invited me to participate in the Dulles colloquium. The Dulles colloquium (named for Avery Cardinal Dulles, who himself attended until shortly before his death) comprises an interesting mix of theologians, philosophers, historians, legal scholars, etc. – Catholic,

---

[14] A promissory note partly redeemed in my forthcoming book, *Ascension Theology*.

Orthodox, Protestant, and Jewish – who meet periodically to discuss books and papers and topics of theological interest. There I encountered the sort of thing that I had missed since leaving the King's Institute, but with a Catholic breadth and a Catholic centre of gravity. As Fr. Richard had no doubt calculated, I not only felt the pull but also became friends with others who were feeling it. In due course, several of us would convert.[15]

My course as an Anglican was not yet run, however, and I had things Anglican on my mind. Or rather I had things Canadian on my mind. The world-wide Anglican communion was by now riven with strife over same-sex blessings, but Canada – at the behest of an Ontario court – had embarked on the path to something called same-sex marriage. Cere and I were among those who realized that this was an affair of far deeper consequence for our country than was commonly thought, and we were soon at work with other colleagues on the Divorcing Marriage book. We had decided to tackle the issue on political, legal and sociological grounds, rather than theological ones, and this occupied a great deal of our attention. But of course it did have theological dimensions, and I naturally continued to think about these in the context of Anglicanism. Eventually I was forced to think about Anglicanism itself in this context, as I will try to explain.

\*

---

[15] Cf. Jason Byassee, "Going Catholic," *The Christian Century*, 22 August 2006, though he does not develop that connection.

The Anglican communion was in visible decline in Britain and North America. Its decline was theological, liturgical, political and numerical, a decline of cogency and even of common sense. One could see it in eminent persons (Desmond Tutu comes to mind) and in obscure or not so obscure places, from the Diocese of Kootenay to the Diocese of London. Archbishop Tutu I did not know personally, but I recall being at a Eucharist he celebrated during a church rally while I was still a student at King's. Clouds of incense filled the cathedral before our great march through the streets of Portsmouth. Tutu didn't march, though he no doubt waved to us as he flew off in his helicopter for God knows where. The next day the headline in the paper read, "Clerics paralyze Portsmouth." I thought that rather funny. Not that I'd expected Tutu to stick around and heal people, but clerics were not meant to paralyze. And now, a decade and a half later, it seemed that the Anglican communion itself was paralyzed.

The presenting symptom of the disease that was paralyzing it was the same that had appeared when the Church of England came into existence: a dispute over the sacrament of marriage. King Henry had resolved the dispute about his own marriage by taking authority over the sacrament itself, or rather by taking authority over the church whose sacrament it was. In Canada the government of Jean Chrétien, though all but paralyzed by its shrinking number of seats in the House – ironically, it was a prominent opponent of same-sex marriage who propped up his government at the eleventh hour just long enough for it to pass Bill C-38, but that's another story – was completing the task Henry had begun. A Catholic prime minister and his Jewish Minister of Justice, with the blessing of the Supreme Court of Canada, were making marriage a mere creature of the State. And Anglicans, who better than anyone else ought to have understood what was happening, were a decade or more behind the curve and convulsing themselves over same-sex blessings.[16]

While C-38 was still in gestation, the Anglican Church of Canada convened its 2004 General Synod under the chairmanship of the new Bishop of Kootenay. Watching on the web, I was moved to write a response, which was published on 6 June by the Anglican Communion Institute. Its title was "Different Gods."[17] In it I expounded the relevance of the 1934 Barmen Declaration to the situation created by the passage of Resolution A-134, which affirmed "the integrity and sanctity of committed same-sex relationships." What I objected to in that resolution was not so much its anthropology or its sexual ethic as its soteriology, which was essentially self-referential. "Commitment" already implied integrity and even sanctity; for that no act of God was necessary, apparently, only an act of man. This was Pelagianism of the

---

[16] Bill C-38, *The Civil Marriage Act*, received royal assent on 20 July 2005. It states that "Marriage, for civil purposes, is the lawful union of two persons to the exclusion of all others." I have written more about these things in *Nation of Bastards*, the epilogue of which addresses the Anglican dilemma.

[17] The text is available at http://www.virtueonline.org/portal/modules/news/article.php?storyid=926.

first order, albeit with a much-diminished element of the asceticism Pelagius himself advocated. I was beginning to see that Pelagianism had become a Protestant pandemic, which no application of the principles of sola gratia and sola fide and sola scriptura seemed capable of stemming. Indeed, I was beginning to wonder whether the latter two slogans, which the Catholic Church has always claimed to be false, necessarily undercut the former, which the Catholic Church believes to be true. Perhaps it was of the nature of Protestantism to be self-referential. What was it Luther was supposed to have said – "Here I stand, I can do no other"?

Later that summer I was invited to speak to a national conference of Anglicans opposed to same-sex blessings, a kind of counter-synod held in Ottawa under the rubric "The Way Forward." One of the organizers was our good friend, Brett Cane, who by now had moved to a parish in Winnipeg. Regrettably, I have to say that The Way Forward was for me the beginning of the way out. Recalling how Colin Gunton had returned to London speaking of a status confessionis, after he had addressed a similar conference held by the United Church of Canada some years earlier, I followed up "Different Gods" with a speech entitled "Ecclesial Existence Today."[18] In "Different Gods" I had concluded by quoting Barth, who drafted the Barmen Declaration.

---

[18] The text is available at http://www.virtueonline.org/portal/modules/news/print.php?storyid=1246. Its title is adapted from Barth's famous book, *Theological Existence Today!*

It is time to face reality. I for one find myself, post General Synod 2004, utterly divided from the Anglican Church of Canada in its present form. Utterly divided not over issues of sexuality, as some vainly imagine, but over something much more serious, as the primates of the global south have recognized. To those responsible for this situation, it is time to say: 'We have different beliefs, different spirits and different Gods.'

In "Ecclesial Existence Today" I again drew on Barth, for if there is an antidote to Pelagianism to be found in Protestantism, where better to look for it? Barth had recognized, even among those who resisted the incursion of National Socialism into church life, a temptation to seek salvation in church politics rather than in Jesus Christ. The same temptation, I believed, now faced Anglicanism:

What is at stake in our own church crisis is not mere formal independence from a body we regard as having lost the authority of the gospel, or from bishops who no longer proclaim the gospel. What is at stake is material dependence on "the one Word of God whom we have to hear, and whom we have to trust and obey, in life and in death" (Barmen). It is quite possible to establish, as we must, some measure of formal independence from, or even to sever all ties with, General Synod; to set up a network of confessing churches and to hope that the wider Anglican communion will recognize this network as its true partner in Canada. But we could do all of that without taking a single step nearer to what we are called to be, namely, the church of Jesus Christ. In fact, we could expend so much energy doing it that we actually lose track of our ecclesial vocation to share in the mission and ministry of Christ. And we could end up – let us heed the warning voices! – no

more than a self-appointed chaplain to socially conservative culture, in much the same way that the Anglican Church of Canada is today no more than an
aspiring chaplain to so-called progressive or "liberal"
culture.

But there was little appetite, it seemed, for anything more than a merely political solution to what
was at bottom a spiritual problem. A pre-conceived
plan for political realignment was hastily modified
to accommodate virtually every degree of compromise. Though the plan adhered to no obvious evangelical principle, and lacked even strategic coherence, it was presented to the assembly and summa-
rily adopted.

I had set out my own view in words that to
some, perhaps, were incomprehensible, and to others simply impractical. They pointed, however, to
something indispensable to any authentically ecclesial way forward, namely, a consideration of the
whole body of Christ:

> It is right that we should renew our own devotion
> to Christian unity. Ecclesial existence today, in the
> face of local and even national apostasy, may indeed
> mean to become more authentically Anglican than we
> have been hitherto, through greater faithfulness both
> to the scriptures and to the Book of Common Prayer.
> It may mean binding ourselves together in renewed
> commitment to the same, even to the breaking of fel-
> lowship with those who have set aside the divine au-
> thority of the one and the rightful governance of the
> other. But if the unity we seek is a unity of the gos-
> pel, if it is a unity authentically Christian – a unity in
> Christ and in the Holy Spirit – then it cannot be a
> merely Anglican unity. This is a time of reckoning
> for us all. How far does our devotion to Christian

unity go, and how consistent is it? If we find warrant
in the gospel for a realignment (to use the popular
euphemism) within Anglicanism, may we not also
find warrant for a realignment of Anglicanism? Of
course, if Anglicanism is mere Protestantism such
questions need not be asked. Fragmentation is our
doom. But insofar as Anglicanism aspires, as in the
Solemn Declaration, to being catholic and apostolic –
a portion of the one church dedicated to the recovery
of ecclesial unity – they are crucial. The ecumenical
implications of decisions about reconfiguration will
have to be considered very carefully, together with
the whole business of Anglicanism's raison d'être.
Anglicanism, at its best, was the best reform movement the sixteenth century could muster. At its worst
it was mere Protestantism, not to say a detour into
rank Erastianism. Humbled by the fact that it now
finds itself a fractured communion, riddled – and not
only in the west – with forms of cultural syncretism
and political servitude as egregious as any Rome and
Orthodoxy have seen, perhaps it is time for Anglicanism to pursue, not its own unity, so much as that of
the church.

The course I was seeking was "a course that
leads the faithful deeper into unity with all who
hold to the Nicene faith and to the Christian way of
life, and who respect episcopal order as far as
possible under the conditions of a church seeking to
overcome its historic divisions," but a different
course would be pursued. I was not the only one to
depart disappointed.

Things were moving quickly now. At the passage of A-134 I had ceased to receive communion
in the Anglican Church of Canada. My family and I
(there were seven of us now) had begun attending
our Catholic parish church, Corpus Christi in

Senneville, where Anna at least was able to receive. On 16 November 2004 I wrote to the rector of St. George's and advised him and the parish family – with sorrow, for we had been involved there for some seven years – that I found it necessary to withdraw from membership. "When we were married," I wrote, "we not only committed ourselves to bringing up our children in the Catholic faith but to being – both in our own family as a 'domestic church' and in the church as such – a part of the bridge between the Anglican and Roman Catholic communions. In our part of the world, that is increasingly difficult to do, and we do not know how to do it any longer except by standing firm and refusing to drift with the Anglican Church of Canada." I also withdrew from formal responsibilities at the Anglican Diocesan Theological College and the Archbishop's Theological Commission.

Things were moving quickly in the worldwide Anglican communion as well. The Windsor Report had been released on 18 October and I was reviewing it for *First Things*. Two things struck me about the report that are germane here. One was the tendency to regard communion in procedural terms and the other was the set of procedural adjustments by which it hoped to strengthen communion. The Windsor Report called for more robust instruments of unity, almost Roman instruments: the Archbishop of Canterbury as chief pastor and teacher, surrounded by a council of advice something like a curia, synods with universal authority, internationally recognized canon law, etc. At the same time it demanded respect for diocesan boundaries and an end to "territorial invasions" by foreign or dissenting bishops. This was Catholicism-lite, so to say, and what was especially "lite" was the substance of the catholic faith; for there was no basic agreement, either in the Windsor Report or on the ground, as to what that faith is. That the report should make such recommendations, without even asking whether it was credible to reconceive Anglicanism in these global or universal terms, as a kind of shadow-Catholicism, was, as far as I could see, "theologically and ecumenically irresponsible." The good ship Anglican, I opined, would be well advised to put in at the nearest Roman harbour, pick up a copy of *Ut unum sint*, and attempt to reset its navigational equipment.[19]

That, at all events, was what I had determined to do myself. I saw no way now to justify adherence to the local Anglican bishop (himself surely the product of a "territorial invasion") over the Catholic bishop. I knew all too well, of course, that more than a few Anglicans thought adherence to their bishop merely a matter of convenience, and that many, when push came to shove, would resort to congregationalism. Indeed, several close friends had already done so. But that was not something I could

---

[19] The review appeared in the January 2005 issue under the title "Anglicanism runs aground." I am conscious now, as I was then – for I remained in conversation with Tom Wright – that it is quite possible to put the report in a more favourable light; but it revealed to me, in a way that nothing else had, the contradiction at the heart of Anglicanism.

do. Congregationalism seemed to me to be inherently self-referential and more or less blind to the problem of church unity. And did it not entail a falsification, if not actual abandonment, of the sacraments? Neither, however, could I decide to become a Catholic merely as a refugee from Anglicanism, as if the Catholic Church were simply a charity of some sort. My own navigational equipment, ecclesiologically speaking, would have to be reset.

*

One of my many fond memories of Colin Gunton dates back to the 1989 conference of the Society for the Study of Theology, at Exeter College in Oxford, where we were listening to a paper on "Prayer and Theological Integrity" by Rowan Williams. At one point he leaned over to me and whispered with a mischievous grin, "Just another Welsh pietist!" Colin, alas, died suddenly just two months after Williams (pietist or not) became the 104th Archbishop of Canterbury, but I doubt that the appointment surprised him. For his own part, Colin was a congregationalist, who served humbly as an associate minister in his beloved Brentwood United Reformed Church. He was also a trinitarian theologian with a keen interest in the ontology of communion; hence his intellectual partnership with John Zizioulas. Both men rejected individualism in all its varieties and were also wary of the exaggerated institutionalism that is individualism's opposite pole. Colin suspected Anglicanism of both sins. Ecclesiologically, however, or at all events ecclesiastically, he and Zizioulas were themselves almost at opposite poles. I have already said that congregationalism was no more an option for me than the Anglicanism Colin had always doubted, and that I too now doubted. But what, then, of Orthodoxy? Might I, ought I, consider looking for a home among the Orthodox?

I recalled being with John of Pergamon that same year (1989) at St. John the Baptist Monastery in Tolleshunt Knights. So bewildered was I by the liturgical complexity of what was going on around me that I didn't even notice him motioning me to come forward to receive the antidoron. But bewilderment is a passing hindrance, and the wealth of the eastern liturgy, theology, iconography and spirituality beckoned. I also recalled being, much more recently, in an elevator at the Warwick in Houston with a couple of converts to Antiochian Orthodoxy, who were sharing in a seminar organized by my new friend, Professor Tristram Engelhardt Jr.[20] There was also a Catholic or two in the elevator, and the brief conversation went something like this: Said one of the Orthodox to one of the Catholics: "It is true, is it not, that Rome recognizes Orthodox sacraments as valid?" "Yes," came the reply. "And it is also true, is it not, that among the Orthodox there are serious doubts about Rome?" The reply was again in the affirmative, though this time a little warier. The conclusion that followed from these premises came as quickly as the floor on which the Catholics

---

[20] The topic of the seminar was "Early Reflections on the Dialectic of Freedom and Determination." Cassian was offered as an antidote to Augustine but by now (this was 2004) my appreciation of Augustine was waxing not waning. Cassian I found unpersuasive.

would gratefully retreat to their rooms: "All things considered, then, wouldn't it be safer to be Orthodox?"

The conversation, though it lacked as a proselytization technique something not lacking at the patriarchal stavropegic monastery in Essex, didn't stop me from sharing the antidoron that Sunday at St. George Antiochian Orthodox Church in Houston. Neither did the ethnic factor (exacerbated, some say, rather than ameliorated by the growing numbers of earnest American converts) prove decisive in my turning Romewards. What prevented me from considering Orthodoxy more closely, its sacramental validity notwithstanding, was the same thing that would have prevented me from reverting to congregationalism even had it not lacked sacramental validity. I mean the question of the Petrine ministry, which now impressed itself upon me as a very real and unavoidable problem.

I had taken to heart John Paul II's encyclical *Ut unum sint*, which revealed the burden that in a certain sense defined his pontificate. I had begun examining the ecclesiology of the two Vatican councils.[21] I was convinced that Anglicanism was unconvincing, both historically and theologically, and that Orthodoxy, while profoundly compelling, could not by itself sustain the catholic unity for which the church, in the spirit of

---

[21] *On commitment to Ecumenism* (1995); cf. Richard John Neuhaus, *Catholic Matters*, p. 69. See also my "Church, Ecumenism, and Eschatology" (chap. 19 in Jerry Walls, ed., *The Oxford Handbook of Eschatology*).

Christ's own 'high priestly' prayer, longed. I did not believe that the credal marks of the church were merely eschatological aspirations, as certain evangelical Protestants seemed to think; or that they had yet to be achieved by the march of progress, as many liberal Protestants fancied. I did believe that I myself was responsible to act consistently with the prayer of Jesus and so to take up the challenge of *Ut unum sint*, and I saw no other way to do that, in my own circumstances, than to become a Catholic.

Unless, of course, Catholicism were itself the problem. If it were, then the problem lay either in the way the Petrine office had been conceived and exercised or in the very claim to such an office. But if in the claim itself, then the great majority of Christians, past and present – including many non-Catholics – had been hoodwinked. Not to put too fine a point on it, the great gap theory was right after all. Indeed, Jack Chick was right after all, and Ian Paisley too. You can't claim to be the vicar of Christ, if you're not the vicar of Christ, without being an antichrist. Peter, yes or no? That was the question, and it was a question for every non-Catholic, myself included. Paisley, by the way, I had once heard in a pub (on another subject) and he was not unimpressive. But even putting for Paisley the humblest of Protestants – who would certainly not describe the pope as antichrist – this was no contest. It was not even a reasonable question. That popes can and have behaved like antichrists is difficult to dispute. The view that popes are antichrists, if held by a properly informed person, is schismatic sectarianism of the gravest sort.

Suppose, however, that the problem lay not in the claim itself but in the way the office was exercised. I was sensitive to the Zizioulan critique of Latin ecclesiology, and I had not forgotten my own characteristically Protestant critique in Ascension and Ecclesia – even if I had turned that critique back on Protestantism itself before the book was done. Was it not possible that the Petrine mandate, "feed my sheep, take care of my lambs," had not only been neglected from time to time but misunderstood and misapplied? And, if so, what then? One still ought to recognize the shepherd and seek the unity of the sheepfold. But could one do so, with integrity, as a sheep not quite shorn of its Protestant wool, or ought one to remain outside the fold, looking in, until convinced that the shepherd knew his business?

If all this sounds to my fellow Catholics impossibly hubristic, perhaps it was. Or perhaps it was simply my own experience of the uncertainty of the "separated brethren": the uncertainty that arises whenever they remember, on the one hand, that they are separated and that they don't want to be; and, on the other, that their separation, whether they be Orthodox or Protestant, was not entirely their own fault or their own doing, as the Catholic Church has acknowledged.

*

I was entangled now on the horns of a dilemma, at once practical and theological. On the practical level, I was an excommunicate Anglican:

disciplined not by a body apparently incapable of discipline, but by a self-imposed fast in a context where even the Eucharist provided no definition to the body such as discipline requires. I had gone so far as to accuse the Anglican Church of Canada of apostasy and of an antichristic spirit, but I did not wish to remain excommunicate, as Kierkegaard had when confronting the drift of his Danish church into a subtler kind of apostasy.[22] I was already engaged in a Catholic parish and asking myself why, when real food and drink were set before me, I was unable to partake. The answer was not complicated. I had not properly recognized (though I greatly respected) the Bishop of Rome, who presided over the unity of the Catholic Church. In sorrow and in hope, therefore, I was being disciplined by a body definite enough, and generous enough, to administer discipline.

On the theological level, my dilemma was more complex, and I will try to spare the reader much of its complexity. I must say something, however, in order to make plain the personal crisis into which I was now plunged by the problem of the Petrine ministry. I acknowledged the existence of a Petrine ministry and its most obvious implications respecting the nature and development of the church, the relation of scripture and tradition, the proper goal of ecumenism, etc. I understood that it had implications for how scripture was to be read and how theology ought to be done; that all these things were to

---

[22] Kierkegaard himself considered turning to Rome, but his circumstances were very different and he did not do so.

be governed by a communion that was not merely notional but real, and not merely occasional but institutional. I recognized that a magisterium existed and must be heeded. But I had a problem. I still had reservations about certain things taught by the magisterium. Were I already a Catholic that problem – which is common enough! – would present itself differently. Were I not a theologian the solution might be to plead ignorance or incompetence and leave the solution to others. But I was a theologian who wished to become a Catholic and I feared that I would be asked to confess what I could not (even allowing for a degree of ignorance) in good conscience confess. For in the rite of reception the candidate says: "I believe and profess all that the holy Catholic Church believes, teaches, and proclaims to be revealed by God."

When Pico was charged with entertaining heretical ideas – remarkably few, in fact; only a baker's dozen among the nine hundred theses he posted for debate in Rome were judged to be heretical – he retired to Florence. Much as I would have liked to do that myself, it wasn't an option. I sought instead the counsel of two other converts, Richard Neuhaus and R. R. Reno, when we were together in New York. With the latter, who had entered into communion with Rome only a couple of months earlier, I afterwards engaged in an extensive correspondence about my theological dilemma. Rusty gave as generously of his time as Fr. Richard had of his whiskey. We wrote back and forth, almost daily, about authority and infallibility, about assent and reservation, about first- and second-order dogma, about the impact of schism on the formation of dogma, about the meaning of *Lumen Gentium*'s famous phrase, *subsistit in*,[23] about the potential effect of advances in under-developed areas of magisterial teaching – especially eschatology – on concepts like transubstantiation or on dogmas like the assumption of Mary. We knew, of course, that this exchange was far from the ordinary course of events in a conversion. We knew, too, that we were not trying to settle these issues for ourselves, much less for the church, and that genuine assent could only begin, like Mary's, in humility. As Rusty had said in rendering an account for *First Things* of his own conversion, the church did not need our ideas. But we knew also that a theologian (even in the impoverished academic sense of that word) came as a theologian when he came to say, "I believe and profess all that the holy Catholic Church believes, teaches, and proclaims to be revealed by God."

On the last day of November, Rusty ventured this somewhat Jesuitical conclusion: "I think that you can be received if you have the material

---

[23] "This is the one Church of Christ which in the Creed is professed as one, holy, catholic and apostolic, which our Saviour, after His Resurrection, commissioned Peter to shepherd, and him and the other apostles to extend and direct with authority, which He erected for all ages as 'the pillar and mainstay of the truth'. This Church constituted and organized in the world as a society, subsists in the Catholic Church, which is governed by the successor of Peter and by the Bishops in communion with him, although many elements of sanctification and of truth are found outside of its visible structure. These elements, as gifts belonging to the Church of Christ, are forces impelling toward catholic unity." (§8).

intention to hold the Church's teaching as true doctrine. That which you actually hold, in your mind, as true, will, of course, depend upon the subjective conditions unique to your education, your personality, and your sensibilities. Nearly all people received into the Church do not, in fact, hold the truths taught by the church as true, largely because they simply do not know the dogmas. In your case, it is quite possible to intend to accept a dogma as true while failing to hold it as true, either because of your failure to understand the meaning of the dogma, or because of your inability to square the dogma with other dogmas that you currently hold as true. Your being received into the Church would entail a religious commitment to continue to act upon the intention to come to hold such doctrine as true. The analogy is found in the baptismal pledges, which are statements of intent rather than reports upon one's objective cognitive or moral condition." I was comforted, but not entirely satisfied.

I kept talking and praying with Anna, and consulted with Dan Cere as well. On 27 December 2004, just about the time the new issue of *First Things* appeared carrying my response to Windsor, I wrote to Bishop Anthony Mancini (now Archbishop of Halifax, then Vicar General in Montreal) expressing my desire to be received into communion, whatever my remaining questions and partly resolved struggles. It was the feast of St. John the Apostle and Evangelist, but I evoked St. Cyprian:

> I come as one who has been much edified by study of the Catechism of the Catholic Church and other magisterial documents; who has no doubt about

the primacy of Peter or the call to unity of John Paul
II in *Ut Unum Sint*; who has complete confidence in
the Nicene creed, the gift of the real presence of
Christ in the Eucharist, the power of the Holy Spirit
working through word and sacraments, the communion of the saints, the honour due to Mary, the moral
life as taught by the Church, etc. Nevertheless, I
come also with some of the reservations an Anglican
might be expected to have; as one who (like our Mel-
kite brethren, for example) believes that the Church
has suffered wounds and limitations under the conditions of ancient schism and that these, even where
they touch on doctrine or polity, need to be addressed
in the spirit of *Ut Unum Sint*. It may be the case that
this will cause some to welcome me with reservations, but not, I hope, to refuse me welcome... I make
my request in the spirit of St. Cyprian: 'To God, the
better offering is peace, brotherly concord, and a
people made one in the unity of the Father, Son and
Holy Spirit.'

Bishop Tony responded promptly and kindly
agreed to meet with me in the new year. He even
read "Different Gods" and "Ecclesial Existence
Today." I wondered what further assurances he
might want from me, beyond my letter, respecting
my understanding and acceptance of the Catholic
faith.[24] He asked, of course, about my reservations.
While he did not seem much troubled by the brief
elaboration I offered, he did want to know whether I
took papal authority seriously. I answered

---

[24] The reference in my letter to the moral life included an
allusion to church teaching on contraception. While I did not
expect to be asked about that (nor was I) I was ready if
asked. Even as an Anglican I had come to understand that
this teaching was true and had accepted the responsibility to
conform to it.

affirmatively. Wisely, he also wanted assurance that I was not turning Romewards for greener pastures – that I was suffering no illusion respecting the state of the Catholic Church, especially in our part of the world. I wasn't. Indeed, I already knew more than I wanted to about the problems that beset the Catholic Church. We agreed that I should proceed toward reception, after further ministry from him in spiritual preparation through the sacrament of reconciliation.

Not surprisingly, perhaps, my struggle now intensified into a crisis. I found myself poring over Lumen Gentium, looking for a way to speak those words from the rite of reception with a clear conscience, and wondering how I could continue with integrity my theological work, the roots of which ran deep into the critical eschatology of Ascension and Ecclesia. "Sometimes I think I see a way forward," I confided to Rusty, "but mostly I find myself between the Rock and a hard place. This morning I got very angry, over very little, with one of my sons, and when alone again found myself weeping almost uncontrollably. I feel like I am faced with a choice between being outside the Church (which cannot be) or giving up my theological vocation, over which I have wept before when I found it too difficult and wished I could give it up. Pray for me, that I do not now go astray."

He did pray, as did Anna, Vincent, and Barbara, the Ceres, Fr. Richard, and many others. Their prayers were answered. I met with our parish priest, Fr. Lou Cerulli, and the Lord ministered to me also through him. My anxiety passed, and peace began to take its place. Bishop Tony had promised to post to me what I required from the RCIA. I smiled when I opened the envelope and found only the rite of confirmation, which I would happily repeat every Sunday were it proper to do so.[25] I smiled again on the day of my confirmation when I was asked to sign the Nicene Creed – nothing more, nothing less – in proof of my coming profession that "I believe and profess all that the holy Catholic Church believes, teaches, and proclaims to be revealed by God." Of questions, I had more and more; of reservations that mattered, I had none.

*

Bishop Tony received and confirmed me at the Newman Centre, with Fr. Peter Sabbath (a Jewish convert, recently ordained, who also had been instrumental in our family pilgrimage) and Fr. Robert Clark concelebrating at mass. Daniel Cere was my sponsor. To the questions I was asked, I answered honestly, with the answers prescribed. I was now a Catholic, and my communion with what Fr. Richard liked to refer to as "the Church of Jesus Christ most fully and rightly ordered through time" was no longer a partial or impaired communion. It was a joyful occasion, which we continued to celebrate with friends and colleagues at a nearby restaurant.

Three weeks later, on 2 April 2005, I was sitting in the Cere's living room lamenting with the world

---

[25] It isn't, of course, since confirmation, like baptism, takes place but once. Unlike baptism, however, confirmation is recognized as valid only if the person performing it is recognized by the Catholic Church.

the passing of John Paul II. I had never had the privilege of meeting him, though he had once passed by just a few metres from me, during a Good Friday procession in the Roman Forum. I was still a student at the time and still wearing my wooden cross. Had he paused to ask me, "Are you Catholic?" I would have had to say, "No, I'm Anglican." I was glad, somehow, that I could give a different answer now, though one certainly did not need to be a Catholic to feel a deep bond with this man, or to thank God for the remarkable things that had been done through him. John Paul had been used by God, not only to change the world, but to change hearts and minds.

After the election of Cardinal Ratzinger as Benedict XVI, when our attention had returned to the routine, a few enquiries were made in Anglican circles by those who had noted my conversion. Kendall Harmon wrote with a request that I speak to these on his widely read website, and posted my reply:

24 April 2005

Rev. Dr Kendall Harmon, Canon
Theologian, Diocese of South Carolina

Dear Kendall,

Thank you very much for your encouraging note, and for asking about my situation. I have not wished to draw attention to myself, though in due course I expect to have something more to say about what is, by its nature, a public and not merely a private action. At the moment I will say only a little.

I was received into communion with Rome on 12 March 2005, the feast of St. Gregory the Great, after no small struggle of heart and mind, in which I was quietly supported by much-appreciated prayers and theological conversation. I had not received communion in the Anglican Church of Canada since General Synod 2004, for reasons articulated or implied in "Different Gods" and "Ecclesial Existence Today."

I should add that Anna and I were married in the Catholic Church, and it had become very difficult to see how we could hope to serve as a domestic bridge between communions that were drifting ever further apart. We could not but recognize in that drift a fundamental problem for both communions. As I pointed out in *First Things*, the remedies proposed by the Lambeth Commission (remedies, that is, for Anglicanism) seemed only to exacerbate the underlying difficulty.

To change the metaphor: The Catholic mission to England under Gregory has led to an abundance of good fruit down through the centuries, both before and after the western schism. Some of that fruit has sprung up on the Anglican branches of the vine of Christ, not only in England but around the world. Nevertheless, the schism itself has always threatened the integrity of those branches and the health of the fruit.

Divine providence, if I am not mistaken, is drawing this to our attention. It is also pruning Anglicanism of its Erastian commitments and characteristics, whether political or cultural or theological, so that its churches may discover what truly holds them together and where their roots actually lie. I would gladly be of some use in that process of discovery. But I am convinced that the process itself and the answer to which it leads – Jesus Christ! – is one that requires repentance for the schism and a willingness to recognize once again the ministry of Peter, who knows something himself about pruning and about being pruned.

There is no going forward without going back. For my part, that is what I have done. I am grateful that I was permitted to do it in the final days of John Paul the Great, whose preaching of Christ was used

by God to encourage and instruct me, together with
so many others.

Yours in the peace of Christ,

Douglas Farrow

PS: Did you write to me on the feast of St.
George for a reason? If so, let us venture to invoke
his prayers against the dragon of disunity.

Naturally the news was not everywhere well received. Reactions ranged from the wistful to the
bemused. One dear friend, to whom I had written a
brief note, responded with evident disappointment
and a couple of pointed questions: "How many of
the 'Roman' elements of Roman Catholicism can
you really sign up for? Does this mean that we can
no longer participate in the Eucharist together –
recognising our acceptance by grace in the sole
priesthood of Christ and as members of the one
body? I appreciate that the Anglican communion
has its problems, but now is just the time when it
needs the kind of theological leadership you are
able to offer." I had not had opportunity to explain
to him very much of what I have set down here, and
I did not think to reply that I was offering, even to
my Anglican brethren, the only kind of leadership I
knew how to give. But drawing on our common
appreciation for Barth, I reminded him that Barth
had mused at the end of his life about the possibility
that one day the voice of the Good Shepherd might
find "a clearer echo" in Rome than in the Reformed
churches. "That day has come," I said, "if I have not
gone completely deaf." I also pointed out that what
I had signed up to, in the presence of a priest and

two witnesses, was precisely the Nicene Creed, which no longer governed the Anglican Church of Canada.

The problem of Eucharistic communion was one I felt keenly, however. I had experienced this pain from the outside myself; now I felt it from the inside. But though I knew, as did he, that we were still bound together by virtue of our common baptism in the royal priesthood of Jesus Christ, and that disunity among the baptized displeased God, I also knew, as did he, that disunity could not be overcome by ignoring the question of holy orders; that is, of the ministerial priesthood and of Peter's role in the oversight and maintenance of that priesthood. The question of authority had to be faced in and with the question of communion. "If you are asking me whether I believe that the unity of the church, in the sense of its visible unity on earth, is intended by our Lord to be sustained by the ministry of Peter, the answer is yes."

Recalling that brief exchange, perhaps unsatisfactory to my friend, puts me in mind of Augustine's claim that "there is nothing more wholesome in the Catholic Church than using authority before argument."[26] Augustine was thinking like this: Because we are made in the image of the living God, who has and is the fellowship of the Father and the Son in the Holy Spirit, love precedes knowledge, faith precedes reason, and authority precedes argument. (Substitute the word "enables" for the word "precedes", if you like, and that will

---

[26] *On the Morals of the Catholic Church* §47

help you get the picture.) When I was a Protestant I had no difficulty with that,[27] so long as the authority in question was mediated by the scriptures and by preaching; as a Protestant, of course, I resisted the notion that it was mediated by any formal magisterium. To be Catholic, however, is to accept, as I now do, not only that authority precedes argument, but that the church possesses this authority: in its prophets and saints and martyrs, yes, hence in the *sensus fidelium*; in its scriptures and creeds and liturgies, certainly, and even (though less certainly) in its great theological traditions; but also in its living magisterium, in the college of the apostles and their successors, united round Peter and his successors.

Catholics do not think that it is possible to do without a magisterium, or that there is any reason or justification to try, since God has provided one. Nor do they think, as Barth perhaps thought, that the gift of a magisterium is somehow like the gift of prophecy; that it shows itself here and then there, speaking with this voice, then that – as if it were no more than an "echo" bouncing around in the ecclesial crater formed and reformed by the repeated impact of the word of God. Good Catholics, like good Protestants, know that the word of God is living and active, "sharper than any two-edged sword," but also that the church's reception of the word of God is a process of growth, guided by a faculty of judgment invested in the apostolic college with Peter at its head. They believe that, when Jesus said to Peter

---

[27] I had learned it in another form from Barth, who learned it from Anselm.

that he was giving to him the keys to the kingdom, he meant it; and that the survival of the papacy and of the Catholic Church through thick and thin (not unlike the survival of the Jewish people) is a work of God and not merely the work of man.

To be sure, there is a certain kind of convert to Catholicism who is prone to stress above all things the authority of the Catholic Church. I am not such, and do not wish to be taken for such, as Rusty can attest. When it began to appear likely that my confirmation would take place at the Newman Centre, our background conversation turned to Newman. Newman was wrong, I thought, to make the claim that "the essential idea of Catholicism is the Church's infallibility." If Catholicism has an essential idea, it is that God is love. But from that fact it does follow that authority precedes argument, which perhaps was all that Newman had in mind. He was right, in any event, when he said in the same place that "not to submit to the Church is to oppose her;"[28] though we would be wrong to

---

[28] The quotation is from *Lectures on Certain Difficulties Felt by Anglicans in Submitting to the Catholic Church* (1850), Lecture XII, p. 306; for context, however, see Lecture X, which suggests that I was over-reading Newman's claim. Dan Cere (who has forgotten more about Newman than I have yet begun to know) later pointed out that in *A Grammar of Assent* (1870) Newman takes Gibbon to task for failing to see Christianity – hence also Catholicism, viewed there not as an alternative to Protestantism but as Christianity in its most concrete form – christologically. Newman himself, in other words, would not approve the kind of thinking from which I am here distancing myself. It ought also to be recalled that he adopted a far more nuanced view of infallibility than did Manning, for example, while nonetheless exercising the discipline of unity in responding to Vatican I.

suppose that submission means anything less than participation, according to the measure of the gifts we have been given, in the authority the church has and in the arguments that it conducts. My last word to Rusty before my reception was this: "If I am wrong, as surely I am about all sorts of things, I want to be in the place where I can learn to be right, with and through the church. I am ready to take up my small place in the debate inside the Catholic Church." That, I suppose, is what Ignatius had in mind when he counselled his followers to learn to think with the church, and what Newman also had in mind with his grammar of assent.

\*

Anna and I held our wedding in Oregon so that the Californians (mainly Catholic) and the British Columbians (mainly Protestant) could meet half-way. The idea, which worked splendidly, was that they would get to know each other at St. Rita's for a couple of days before they witnessed our marriage together. Now it so happened that a couple of carloads, one of my relatives and one of hers, arrived at the same time. The occupants of the latter were uncertain as to whether to continue up the dirt road on which they were both travelling in search of St. Rita's. Turning back, and mistaking my sister Helen's husband, Austin, for Anna's maternal grandfather, Dutch Higgs, they rolled down their window and hollered out, "Are you Dutch?" Austin, not knowing that Anna's grandfather had that nickname, replied with some perplexity, "No, I'm Canadian!" After they sorted that out, they went on to their destination together.

The road to heaven is rather longer than the road to St. Rita's, and a witness to much confusion. If it weren't, there wouldn't be labels like Roman Catholic, Orthodox, Anglican and Protestant. These labels, however, concern only the church militant, not the church triumphant – the church on the way, not the church at rest. Where Fr. Richard has lately gone, where my father-in-law, Vincent, and my mother, Kay, have gone, that question is moot. Which is to say, the question "Are you Catholic?" is certainly not the equivalent of the question sometimes asked by Protestants, "Are you saved?" To treat it as such is to embrace a fundamentalism that the church itself rejects, and to mirror that particular Protestant confusion. The one church of Jesus Christ "subsists in the Catholic Church," says Lumen Gentium, yet not all who belong to Christ reside or labour within the visible communion of the Catholic Church, nor has the Spirit of God limited his ecclesial work to her.

Neither, however, is the question "Are you Catholic?" like the question "Are you Dutch?" or "Are you Canadian?" It directs us to something of far greater significance than our national, or even our global, citizenship in the city of man. It directs us to our citizenship in the everlasting city of God as that city expresses itself in the saeculum. It enquires after the concreteness of our unity in Christ, after the fullness of the church and of its witness to the world. It points us to the ministry of Peter, one of whose tasks it is to address (from experience!) the confusion that arises on the road. In the years since the question was first put to me I have come to believe that, for the sake of that unity and that fullness and that witness, "Yes" is the best answer to give. I have tried to give it in a way that is authentically Catholic and not still secretly Protestant, while rejoicing over the many gifts I have received from Protestant and from Orthodox hands. "And now that we've sorted that out," I can hear Fr. Richard saying, "let us travel on together."

# Ian Hunter

Dr. Ian Hunter is Professor Emeritus in the Faculty of Law at Western University. He is the author of several books, including biographies of Malcolm Muggeridge, Hesketh Pearson, and Robert Burns. He lives in St. Thomas, Ontario.

## My Path to Rome

It is difficult to write objectively about something as intensely personal as conversion; I recognize also that my own conversion is but one case among many, but since it is the one I know best, it is what I shall try here to explain.

Let me dare to begin with a question that perhaps should best come last: What is the alternative to conversion? – except what G. K. Chesterton, writing of his own conversion, called a sorry surrender to "...the awful actualities of our time"? I came to believe that there is no answer, except Rome, to that question.

Still it is legitimate to ask: why someone, in the sixth decade of his life, with more of life behind than ahead of him, would abandon his denomination and the liturgies and traditions with which he is familiar, for the remote, somewhat intimidating vastness of Rome? In short, why become a Roman Catholic?

110

Well, all such stories are long ones, and just as aspects of one's human birth remain mysterious, so also aspects of one's spiritual rebirth, perhaps opaque beyond human explanation. But here is what I know. My conversion story is, in part, the story of four men, only two of whom were Catholics.

But before I tell you about the part played by these four men, let me say something about how I experienced the mechanics of becoming a Roman Catholic.

I first tried the RCIA program a few years ago at a London Catholic church and I found that experience quite disillusioning. At the first meeting there were a handful of people (mostly young girls taking instruction because they were engaged to Catholic boys), and the course leader, an extremely friendly woman whose purpose, so far as I could discern, was to make us understand just how very special and wonderful each one of us really and truly was; soon, she said, we would become "really, really close" and there was much group hugging – at least metaphorically – but little instruction on matters of Catholic doctrine. Needless to say, the word "dogma" was never used. Now since I had gone to learn more about Catholic dogma, I found the leader's forced intimacies embarrassing, the pabulum offered un-nourishing, and the absence of discussion unsatisfactory.

After going to a few of the weekly sessions, I dropped out; when I was attending I noted that on the rare occasions when Catholic doctrine was mentioned, it was usually misstated (using the Catechism of the Catholic Church – itself never mentioned – as the standard), or deferred. So if a difficult question was raised, say, about Catholic teaching on marriage or purgatory, the response would be: "Oh, we'll get to that". Then we would be reassured again how close, how intimate, how loving, we all were; I confess that I left the group before any such intimacy could flourish.

By the spring of 2005, as Pope John Paul II lay dying in Rome, I had moved to St. Thomas, Ontario, and I went to the main-street, downtown, gothic Catholic Church, Holy Angels, to pray for the Pope in what were clearly his last days on earth.

On the actual day that he died, a Saturday (April 2, 2005) there was an afternoon mass at Holy Angels and I went. The grief among the congregation was palpable. But to my astonishment, the priest carried on as though nothing whatever had happened; only when he came to the prayers of the people did he mention in passing that since the Holy Father had just died, we would be skipping the prayer for the Pope. Otherwise, nothing. When the announcements came, we were reminded of an upcoming pot luck dinner and other social events, but not a word to assuage the shared grief that was palpable in the congregation; then we were dismissed, orphaned as I thought, into the night.

I was not then a Catholic. But I considered John Paul II the brightest light in the dark times through which I had lived my life, and on that day I expected more. "Never again will I enter this church", I muttered through clenched teeth on the way out the door. But, as often happens, God had other plans.

Which brings me to the first of four men responsible for my becoming a Catholic, by name Karol Wojtyla, a relatively obscure Polish Cardinal who astonished the world when on October 16, 1978 he stepped out on the balcony at St. Peter's, announced his new identity as Pope John Paul II, and declared in a dozen or more languages: "Be not afraid... Open the doors to Jesus Christ!"

In that sense I suppose that I am what might be called "a JP II Catholic"; if so, I am honoured to be called after a man I so much admire. Without the papacy of John Paul II, I doubt I would have been drawn so inexorably to the Roman Catholic Church.

Within a year of John Paul II becoming Pope, I wrote a feature profile for a Canadian newspaper; I concluded it with these words:

"Who could have foreseen that in so little time the strongest voice in the Western world would be that of a man uniquely qualified by personal experience to speak to both halves of a world split asunder?"

A year later, on the Pope's first U. S. visit, he met President Jimmy Carter at the White House; at that time I wrote of the strange contrast between the two men: "...the Pope four years older than the President but exuding virility and integrity, a man at peace with himself, and the President, anxiety, uncertainty and indecision written in the lines across his face...".

I went on: "This Pope speaks to the people of eternal verities, truths that in their hearts they know to be true however much they might twist and turn and seek to evade them. Unpalatable truths, articles of faith in an era of rationality, hard sayings in respectable liberal circles, truths that have become particularly embarrassing when it is not only the emperor but all his subjects who have no clothes on. But truths for all that, the kind that sear the conscience and find an understanding and assent that is more instinctual than intellectual".

With growing admiration I watched John Paul II discharge the duties of his office, including his worldwide pilgrimages – especially the triumphant homecoming to Poland. Wherever he went, I noticed how he confounded the ecumenists and pluralists. He appeared always cheerful; he listened attentively, he exuded warmth and compassion. But his words were blunt and uncompromising, so much so that they startled even those like me who had longed to hear such things said: "Do not be afraid of the truth". "Human life is forever", he said. On the ordination of women? No. On abortion: No. On marriage: Indissoluble. On celibacy: Yes. On priestly vows: Forever. This was a man who clearly knew his faith and his mind and was not afraid to speak unequivocally about either.

The main reason why Pope John Paul II was so significant in my conversion is that without his pontificate I doubt that I would have wrestled with the ecclesiological claims that the Roman Catholic Church makes. Ecclesiology might seem an arcane subject, but for me it was pivotal. Yet nothing in my family background or upbringing would have prompted me to reflect on it. Just the opposite, in fact.

Which brings me to the second influential man in my story, my father. My father, James Hogg

Hunter, was born in 1890 in Maybole, Scotland – in the Covenanting district of Scotland where men and women died as martyrs to the Protestant faith. Two of my father's novels (How Sleep the Brave (1955) and The Hammer of God (1965)) are about the persecution of Scottish Covenanters. My father was a Presbyterian and among his bedrock beliefs was the conviction that Rome was the enemy of the Christian faith. It is difficult to communicate today the depth and sincerity of his conviction.

My father immigrated to Canada in the early part of the 20$^{th}$ century, and he spent the next six decades engaged in Christian journalism, primarily as Editor of a monthly magazine called "The Evangelical Christian". In its pages he denounced "...Popery in all its forms" and, as he put it "...sought to expose the shams and deceits of this 'Mystery of Iniquity', the Roman Catholic Church."

The zenith of my father's anti-Catholic polemics was his 1945 book, The Great Deception, a book that would be banned today as hate literature. Lest you think I exaggerate, here is a taste of what lies within its covers; I quote here from the Preface:

"There are people who know little of the history and the dark deeds of this system [Roman Catholicism], this mystery of iniquity that has stood through the centuries, not because it was founded on the Rock of Ages, but because it is part of the inscrutable permissive will of God. Why God should have suffered this gigantic imposture to continue is not for us to discuss or explain, any more than it is ours to account for the religion of Mohammedanism or any other of the many false cults and religions that abound in the world. We believe with the Reformers that the rise, history and doom of the Roman Catholic Church is set forth in the Book of Revelation, and that when the hour of God strikes it will be destroyed. It is not the saving Gospel of sovereign grace that is set forth by the Church of Rome, but a travesty of that great truth; not the religion of the Lord Jesus Christ but that of the anti-Christ; not the faith once delivered to the saints, but a caricature of that faith – a deep and awful delusion that is ruining souls."

I quote that passage ruefully, not to mock or disparage my father, a fine and dear Christian man whom I loved, but rather to demonstrate how broad the chasm it was necessary for me to cross in order to come to Rome. Yet when I consider who played a part in my decision, my father is near the top of the list, and I'll tell you why: he took religion seriously. In fact his faith was the most important thing in his life. For him Christianity was not a convenience but a life creed; attending church was not a social outing but an opportunity to worship in the presence of Almighty God; religion was not a subject for social chatter, but a life-changing commitment.

I had already written that when I came across this passage by Thomas Howard, like me a late convert to Catholicism, who came from a similar protestant evangelical background; Howard writes:

"...it is to Protestant Fundamentalism, ironically, that I owe my having at last found my way into the Church, for it was the Fundamentalists, most notably my father and mother, who taught me the apostolic faith. They taught me that there is nothing – nothing at all for one's attention – that may be compared to the excellency of the knowledge of Christ Jesus the Lord. They instilled in me the immense gravity of the matter, that to obey and serve God must swallow up all other contenders. And they taught me, I think, that the peace and order both in one's inner man and in one's household, that follow upon such obedience and service, are a treasure to be desired and sought most sedulously. Everything else is ultimately illusionary, fugitive, and perfidious." (*On Being Catholic*, Ignatius Press, 1997, p. 11)

Because he took his faith seriously, because it was the defining feature and centre of my father's life, I wonder sometimes what – had he lived to survey the ruins of Protestantism, where mainline churches like the Anglican and United Church compete in bringing ridicule upon the faith he cherished – he would have done; given this sorry spectacle, might he not have made a similar pilgrimage to Rome? I wonder, but can never know.

So I have told you about two of the influences on my conversion: Pope John Paul II and my father.

The third influence could be considered a paradox since he never himself became a Roman Catholic; I refer to C.S. Lewis. All my Christian life I have been reading and learning from C.S. Lewis's books; particularly to pick three – Mere Christianity, Surprised by Joy, and The Great Divorce.

The distinguished American novelist, Walker Percy, once remarked on the countless converts who had come to Catholicism through the writings of C.S. Lewis: Walker Percy wrote: "….[in stories told by Catholic converts] writers one might expect, from Aquinas to Merton, turn up. But guess who turns up most often? C.S. Lewis."

Yet Lewis himself never converted; he lived, and died (in November 1963) a lifelong Anglican.

In 1999 Joseph Pearce wrote a book called *Literary Converts*, a study of the veritable stampede to Rome of English authors and intellectuals in the 20th century; men like G. K. Chesterton, Ronald Knox, Evelyn Waugh, J. R. R. Tolkien, and Malcolm Muggeridge. I reviewed *Literary Converts* when it came out and nominated it as the best Christian book of the year. More recently Pearce wrote another book, this one called C.S. Lewis *and the Catholic Church* (Ignatius Press), and I reviewed that too. In this book Pearce tries to find the answer to the Lewis paradox; namely why has C.S. Lewis influenced so many Catholic converts and yet never himself became a Catholic?

Despite Pearce's diligent research, and his insightful and balanced reflections, the answer, I believe, eludes him. Pearce's answer – that Lewis was never able to shake off his virulently anti-Catholic Belfast upbringing – I consider unconvincing. I know that kind of upbringing: I experienced something not altogether different myself. It is an obstacle, unquestionably, but not insurmountable.

I believe that the answer is much simpler: in the nineteen forties, fifties and early sixties, when Lewis lived and his influence was at its height, it was still possible to regard the Church of England (particularly in its Anglo-Catholic manifestations)

118

as part of that "…one holy, catholic, and apostolic church" that all Christians, when they recite the Nicene Creed, profess to believe in.

Today, such a belief requires self-deception, or at least wilful blindness. In his time Lewis was spared the spectacle of what the Anglican Church has become, with Bishop Michael Ingham devising rites for same sex unions, while New Hampshire Bishop Vicki Gene Robinson abandons his wife and children to take up with a homosexual lover. In short, in C.S. Lewis's time, the Anglican Church was not yet the self-parody it has become.

Walter Hooper, Lewis's confidante, editor and biographer, sometime Anglican priest, and most assiduous keeper of the Lewis' flame, in 1988 converted to Catholicism. He believes, and has said publicly, that Lewis would do likewise were he alive today. And Lewis's long-time friend, Christopher Derrick, said in 1996: "It's difficult to imagine what Lewis would make of today's Church of England. The Church of England is such a pathetic ghost nowadays …You can't agree with it or disagree with it. There's just nothing there."

If C.S. Lewis was alive today, he would almost certainly be a Roman Catholic. That is the short answer – and, I believe, the most convincing answer – to the Lewis paradox. When I discovered that I believed that, then my last feeble justification for remaining an Anglican – "If it was good enough for C.S. Lewis, then its good enough for me" – was gone. I believe now that anyone who reads and understands Lewis is on the path to Rome.

And so I come to the last, and perhaps most important influence, Malcolm Muggeridge.

In 1966, when I was a law student at U. of T. law school and should have been spending my time immersed in statutes, regulations and cases in the law library, I was more often ensconced in the periodical stacks at Central Library reading Malcolm Muggeridge's prolific journalism.

I had stumbled across Muggeridge quite by chance and was at first struck by his eloquent, wry, effortlessly readable prose, so clear, pungent, and often devastating. His skeptical mind and loathing for cant were a welcome purgative to the academic conversations going on all around me.

I soon exhausted what Muggeridge was available in print. Next came out-of-print books through inter-library loans. Then, via the Index to Periodical Literature, I began working my way backwards through the 1960s, 1950s, 40s, 30s, even into the 1920s, via back numbers of the Guardian, the New Statesman, Time and Tide, and other periodicals. In my third year of law school, I could have answered any question concerning Muggeridge; unfortunately, these were scarce, the examiners preferring instead to test my shaky knowledge of close corporations or the remoter slopes of the Income Tax Act.

I first met Malcolm in the autumn of 1968 when he came to Toronto to give a lecture at the St. Lawrence Centre. On this occasion, I asked him about a short story he had written in India in the early twenties. At first, he barely remembered it, then he said: "Nobody has mentioned that story to me in 50 years! Now we really must talk." He went on to tell me how he had sent such early stories to Mahatma Gandhi who had published them in his newspaper, Young India. Thereupon, Malcolm and I fell into real conversation, and then correspondence, which continued, pretty much uninterrupted, until his death in 1990.

The same year we met, Muggeridge published Jesus Rediscovered, which became an immediate, unlikely bestseller; all of his books from then on dealt with religious themes, including Something Beautiful for God, the book that brought Mother Teresa to worldwide attention.

In 1978-79 Muggeridge and I swapped houses, and for that year I lived in his house in Sussex where I wrote the first biography of Muggeridge. Central to the book was charting his religious pilgrimage, from a Fabian socialist upbringing to his reception, at age 80, into the Roman Catholic Church.

"Rome, sweet Rome, be you never so sinful, there's no place like Rome". So, mockingly, Muggeridge had written in the mid-70s. Yet, on November 27, 1982, Muggeridge knelt before the altar in a chapel in the little Sussex village of Hurst Green and was received into the Catholic Church. When I asked him why, he replied: "The day will come, dear boy, when you must decide whether to die within the church or outside the church. I have decided to die within the Church."

From the day that Malcolm Muggeridge became a Catholic, I thought more seriously of conversion. I remembered how difficult Malcolm's struggle had been and how Mother Teresa had written telling

him to submerge his hesitations in Christ's unbounded love. I especially remembered one of her
letters to him; let me quote it:

> You are to me like Nicodemus '...unless you be-
> come as a little child' ...I am sure that you will un-
> derstand beautifully everything if you would only be-
> come a little child in God's hands. The small diffi-
> culty you have regarding the Church is finite. Over-
> come the finite with the infinite...

So, I have now told you of the four most important, albeit four of many, influences on my decision
to convert: Pope John Paul II, my father, C.S.
Lewis, and Malcolm Muggeridge. But let me return
now to the mechanics, how to get into the Church,
particularly for someone like me who is divorced.

A few years ago, a Catholic friend gave me a
copy of the (then recently-published) Catechism of
the Catholic Church; I was impressed by the depth
and eloquence of it's proclamation of the Christian
faith. This was the faith I affirmed, but which I considered that my own Church no longer did. I wanted
to belong to a Church that published such a splendid
statement of Christian orthodoxy. Despite the disillusioning experience at the Mass on the day of the
Pope's death, it was borne in upon me that Rome
was my spiritual home. But what to do now? I had
tried the RCIA route; it was not for me and I knew
of no other way in.

This brings my narrative to late 2005. I had not
been attending any Church for some months, when
suddenly the conviction overwhelmed me that I
could not properly celebrate the birth of Jesus at

Christmas if I did not worship on the preceding Sundays of Advent. Don't ask me why I was so suddenly convinced of that, I just was. So, on the first Sunday of Advent, expecting another dispiriting experience, I trudged to mass at Holy Angels, the same Catholic Church where I had been disillusioned.

To my surprise, there was a new priest. To my even greater surprise, his homily was directed straight at me. His text was "Come out of the wilderness", and he said something like this: "People experience many kinds of wilderness. There may be someone here who is in a church wilderness, someone who cannot find a church to belong to, or perhaps who has found the church but it is the church to which he cannot belong. To that person Jesus says: 'Come out of the wilderness.'"

The next day, Monday, without calling in advance and without an appointment, I knocked on his door at the Rectory and told him I was the person in the wilderness that he had been referring to. Father Adam Gabriel, (for such is his apt name – and a messenger of God, like his namesake, he has been!) listened to my story and told me about the RCIA program. I told him my past experience with the RCIA. He said that he regretted that he could not give me private instruction, but that Holy Angels is a large, busy parish and he is the only priest; the demands on his time are punishing. Then he noticed that I had brought along my copy of the Catechism of the Roman Catholic Church and he asked me if I had read it? I said that I had. Then he said: "OK. If you are serious enough to have read the Catechism, I'll make the time to give you instruction." And so, over the next year, he did. He also dealt – quietly, thoroughly and effectively – with the other (matrimonial) obstacles to my admission. Needless to say, I owe Father Gabriel an immense debt of gratitude.

So, on July 2, 2006 I was received into the full communion of the Roman Catholic Church, returning not – definitely not as I have already explained – to the religion of my father, but perhaps to the religion of my father's fathers.

Looking back now I see that three considerations became of paramount importance to me: Rome's authority, historicity, and universality. But more even than these considerations, I came to believe not just that truth is to be found within Rome but – something quite different – that in a unique way, the truth is Rome. Incidentally, from within Rome's embrace I did not expect modernity to appear any more comely, but perhaps more bearable. And so it has proved.

Unlike much of Protestantism, Rome is innately suspicious of feelings and enthusiasms; still, the predominant feeling on the day of my reception was of a home-coming, of responding to a bell that I had long heard toll, of taking my place at a table that had long been set, of finding spiritual companionship among those unashamed to profess the faith of the fathers.

I have left the church of my adulthood – the Anglican Church – with mixed emotions; the Anglican ideal, which sought to incorporate the best of the Reformation into Catholicism, still seems to me a worthy – if today unnecessary – goal.

Spiritually, I was nourished by Anglican liturgy, particularly that masterpiece of literature and worship, the Book of Common Prayer; alas, Anglicans today have abandoned the Book of Common Prayer, putting in its place liturgies each one more banal, trite, and politically-correct than its predecessor. Anyway, the more one becomes immersed in the Book of Common Prayer, its 39 Articles, its history, liturgy, and theology, the more inexorably one is drawn to Rome. This is why John Henry Newman memorably described Anglicanism as "…the halfway house on the road to Rome".

I loved, too, the splendid Anglican hymnody, and would be sorry to leave it had it not also been "revised" almost beyond recognition.

I leave with nothing but contempt for what passes for Anglican "leadership", particularly its Bishops, and many of its clerics, those without seeming conviction about matters of doctrine, although erupting regularly with predictable pronouncements about certain social issues; they are "men without chests" (C.S. Lewis's term) when it comes to defending the Christian faith, ministers who have depleted their spiritual patrimony in the vain hope of appearing progressive. By contrast, I have noticed that Rome does not alter its message to suit shifting fashions, nor tailor its doctrine, however persistent or clamorous the public outcry against it may be.

I discovered too that I had grown to believe that only Rome can trace a direct line to the church's rock, St. Peter. It was to St. Peter, after all, and to his descendants, that our Lord promised that the gates of hell would not prevail. Against most churches, the gates of Hell seem to be prevailing very well. Only the Roman Catholic Church, the repository of teaching and traditions that date to our Lord's first disciples, "...the unmoved spectator of the thousand phases and fashions that have passed over our restless world" (to use Ronald Knox's elegant phrase), has the history, the guts, the inner wherewithal, to survive a postmodern age. Rome's claim to speak with authority in matters of faith and morals is the last refuge, or so I now believe, against the all-corrosive acid of postmodernism.

Let me state the position I was in as simply as possible: I came to believe that there is no source of authority outside the Roman Catholic Church. I could abandon the Christian faith, which had nourished me since childhood, or I could submit to and seek membership in the Church which, as St. Paul expresses it "...has the mind of Christ." But there was, for me, no longer any middle ground left.

That doughty old warrior, Hilaire Belloc, once wrote to a friend that the Catholic Church was like a landfall at sea, at first glimpsed hazily and only through the mist: "...but the nearer it is seen, the more it is real, the less imaginary: the more direct and external its voice, the more indisputable its representative character ... The metaphor is not that men fall in love with it: the metaphor is that they discover home. 'This was what I long sought', they say, 'This was my need'."

I owe also a special debt to Catholics, many unknown to me, who I have since discovered had been praying for my reception, some for a long time. Such prayers flood the universe with light. I also acknowledge a Christian reading group to which I have long belonged; in those long droughts when my Church provided little spiritual nourishment ("The hungry sheep look up and are not fed", I used to mutter through clenched teeth on innumerable Sunday mornings), I was invariably fed by these, my Christian brothers.

So, the story of my conversion is the story of four men: Pope John Paul II, my father (albeit, an unwitting guide), C.S. Lewis, and Malcolm Muggeridge. It is the story of the Church's decision to publish a comprehensive Catechism of the Christian faith, and of a priest who willing to go beyond the requirements of his office to fetch one lost sheep out of the wilderness. It is the story of faithful Catholics who prayed. And above all, first, last, and always, it is the same old story that it always is – a story of God's grace and forgiveness and love. Deo gratias.

# Amy Lau

**Amy Lau was born and raised in Ottawa, Ontario, the youngest of three children in her family. After obtaining a M.Sc. in Biochemistry and a B.Ed., she taught for several years in a local high school until she decided to stay at home full-time to raise her growing family. She is married to Tim Lau and presently has five beautiful children.**

## An Inconvenient Truth

L et me preface this chapter by saying I am truly humbled by the present company of distinguished contributors in this book, people living out their Christian vocation with heroism in a world hostile to the Christian faith. I am neither a writer nor an academic. So what could a former high school teacher and currently stay-at-home mother of five children possibly have to say in a book like this? Seems a little out of place. Such was my initial thought when I was asked to write this chapter. This was not the first time I had been asked to share my conversion story beyond the comfort zone of my own circle of friends and my parish. As someone who prefers not to draw attention to herself, I have been, in some ways, like Moses, who tried to avoid God's bidding to go out on a mission, with a 'not me, Lord' attitude. But when the venture was presented to me as 'think of all the good it can do', with prayerful consideration and resignation to God's will, I agreed to share my story with a larger audience, for the sake of God's glory and His Church. Conversion to Catholicism is not reserved for some select group of elite intellectuals. Every conversion story is unique and worthwhile. People need to hear stories like this written by everyday folks, struggling to discern God's will for them and allowing God's amazing grace to work in their lives. For me, it has been a rewarding exercise to reflect back upon my arduous journey into the Catholic Church and how God brought this reluctant soul back home to His fold. In 1 Thessalonians 5:21, St. Paul exhorts us to test everything and hold on to the good. I found goodness, beauty and truth in the place I least expected or wanted to find it. It is my sincere hope that this book will touch people from all walks of life, that they may come to embrace the goodness, beauty and the fullness of the truth as found in the Catholic Faith, as I have done and continue to do, ceaselessly finding precious gems in every corner.

My religious roots are somewhat of a mosaic. Having been raised in an evangelical Protestant faith by a mother whose father was a Buddhist priest in Japan and a father whose parents were generally non-religious (but perhaps culturally Shintoists), not many would have suspected that I would become Catholic in my adulthood. When my parents emigrated from Japan to the United States, they attended a Christian church because back then that was the American thing to do. They even baptized their first baby, my elder sister, in the local Lutheran church. When they moved to Canada where I was subsequently born, they switched denominations because the nearest church in the neighbourhood happened to be Free Methodist. Consequently, I was raised in the Free Methodist church, which today might be considered an 'evangelical' Christian church.

It was my mother who faithfully took me and my siblings to church every Sunday and usually to one or two mid-week activities at the church. I have very fond memories of going to Sunday School, children's clubs, youth groups, summer Christian camps and year-round retreats. It was through these experiences that I received a good grounding in the Bible and in the basic tenets of the Christian faith. And, it is not surprising that many of my friends were Christians when I was growing up. But, most importantly, in this church environment, I was blessed to be surrounded by sincere and devout Bible-believing Christians, including my mother and sister, who loved the Lord with all their heart, soul, mind and strength. Their love for Christ radiated out in the way they lived. This was a powerful witness to the workings of God's grace in their lives.

As was the usual way to become a Christian, I accepted in faith Jesus as my personal Lord and Saviour after 'heeding the altar call' and wholeheartedly 'praying the sinner's prayer'. As a young teen, while at camp, I was baptized in a lake. (In this denomination, baptism was considered a public declaration of faith in Jesus and signified that one had already become a Christian and was a new creation in Christ. Although not everyone was baptized, baptism was highly encouraged since it was commanded by Jesus.) I still remember the joy of emerging from the waters and being greeted with the warm, enthusiastic smiles of fellow Christians, old and new. I truly felt part of the family of God.

Although I was never a strong or model Christian, I was quite convinced that my church denomination and the other evangelical denominations were among the few that were truly Christian. To substantiate my opinion, I looked for 'fruit' as a litmus test for authentic Christianity. As far as I had observed, only the evangelicals seemed to be on fire for the Lord. They were the ones who seemed to be faithfully living out the gospel, and they had a genuine and intimate personal relationship with Jesus. This was in stark contrast to the Catholics, who, in my opinion, seemed to be just going through the motions without any real spiritual life or love for Jesus.

Part of my prejudice stemmed from the fact that I went to the public secular schools while most of the Catholics went to the Catholic schools, thus I had very limited exposure to Catholics when I was growing up. The very few Catholics I had encountered did not at all seem to me to be Christians based on their words and actions, at least not like the fervent kind that I knew from my home church. Catholics drank, smoked, swore, and engaged in licentious behaviour just about the same way (if not more) than the average non-Christian. Unfortunately, Catholics can sometimes give Catholics a bad name.

The other part of the problem was that I was completely ignorant of Catholicism and what the Catholic Church actually teaches. My feeble understanding of Catholicism came from what I witnessed in the media as well as from the personal testimony of people whom I respected and trusted. One of my favourite pastors who served in my church, a gifted preacher and exemplary Christian, was one of those 'fortunate' souls who had been 'saved' from the shackles of Catholicism when someone shared the 'true' gospel of Jesus Christ with him. From his witness and that of others, I was led to believe that Catholicism was a false religion, steeped in superstition and idolatry, and whose teachings and practices were entirely unbiblical. Catholics were not true Christians and sadly they had been deceived into thinking that they were 'saved' merely because they were baptized as infants. Although I had never attended a Catholic mass, I thought that worship in the Catholic Church was ritualistic, superficial, mundane and lifeless. Catholics seemed to be so caught up in works, statues and saints. Catholics prayed to Mary as if she was a god. What about the one mediator between God and man, the Lord Jesus? Even the sight of the crucifix made me uneasy, as all too many evangelical Christians will attest they prefer to focus on the risen Christ rather than dwell on His suffering and death. As with many evangelicals today, I was under the impression that the Catholic Church was a man-made institution that had fallen away from the truth, having distorted and complicated the simple gospel with excessive and vain rituals, burdensome regulations, and unnecessary hierarchical structures. Who needs a pope when we have Christ as the Head of His church, and the Bible and the Holy Spirit to guide us? Although these misguided notions about the Catholic Church were not preached from the pulpit nor were they official teachings of the particular denomination to which I belonged, they reflected the opinions of many evangelicals and unfortunately the ignorance of Catholicism and prejudice against Catholics ran deep in that milieu.

Such was the Christianity of my childhood. Though blissful it was, things changed after high school when my Christian friends went their separate ways. When I began university, I became preoccupied with my studies, my part-time job, and my newly found independence and social life. Away from a protective circle of Christian influences and increasingly surrounded by non-Christians and the secular mentality of the current culture, I was soon enticed by the so-called pleasures of the world. The impact of these diversions had an all too familiar result, as with many young adults of today: I stopped going to church and I strayed far from God.

But God was not finished with me yet. In the middle of my undergraduate years, I started dating a non-Christian young man named Tim. He was an 'unchurched' fellow, meaning that he was never raised in any faith. Although I was not a practising Christian at the time, I found it difficult to see eye-to-eye with Tim on many issues, social and moral. We had a turbulent relationship but somehow we stayed together, even throwing around the idea of future marriage in our minds. A few years into our relationship, however, I plunged into an emotional and spiritual low. My life divorced from God had taken its toll. I started feeling the need to reconcile with God and I wanted to be close to Him again, but this was going to be difficult with my non-Christian boyfriend in the picture. Yet with the busyness of completing my undergrad studies and still being attached to things of the world, I put those feelings on hold.

Miracle of miracles: Who would have thought that God would use a non-Christian to bring a fallen-away Christian back into relationship with God and later into the fullness of the Catholic faith? It was actually through encountering several devout Catholics whom Tim was to befriend that I would rejuvenate my faith, only later to be led along a path I never thought I would go (but thanks be to God I eventually did!).

It was at the beginning of our graduate studies that something was stirring in Tim – he must have been ripe for the workings of the Holy Spirit. Tim started expressing an interest in Christianity! How on earth did this happen? Tim's thesis supervisor had apparently been sharing intriguing stories with Tim during lunchtime. Tim would later find out that these stories were actually parables of Jesus. This professor of Tim's was a Catholic, a very warm person with a serenity of one who truly abandons himself to God. I was rather impressed by this Catholic who actually knew something about the Bible (I did not think Catholics even owned a Bible let alone read one). Moreover, I was delighted that Tim desired to know more about God. This was the catalyst that spurred me on to return to the faith of my childhood. I was relieved that I no longer had to hide from Tim my desire to return to God. I started praying and reading the Bible again. The icing on the cake came when Tim agreed to try attending the evangelical church I grew up in. I was overjoyed that we could now journey in our faith together in the church of my upbringing. We started attending Sunday services and small group Bible studies together at my old church. We enjoyed the warm, fervent atmosphere and we were making some wonderful Christian friends. It was truly a happy time for me and on the surface it seemed so for Tim. However, as I would soon find out, something was not quite sitting well with him.

Tim's professor had been introducing him little by little to the Catholic faith. I soon began hearing from Tim what the Catholic Church has to say about this and about that. It started to get annoying but I figured Tim was just comparing Catholicism with evangelical Protestantism and would eventually embrace the beauty of the Christian faith as expressed in my church. I was not hostile to the Catholic Church at this point – I probably did not think it was as sinister as I had originally suspected, especially since now I had met at least one Catholic who seemed to be a Christian. Nevertheless, I still viewed the Catholic Church as an unbiblical, man-made institution, fraught with errors and scandal, and consequently I was extremely leery of its teachings.

However, God would continue to peel the scales from my eyes and warm me up to the Catholic Church by planting more faithful Catholics along the way. As Tim was preparing for medical school, his professor introduced us to a Catholic physicians' guild which met monthly to discuss medical ethics from a Catholic standpoint. The first time I attended one of those meetings, it was an incredibly awkward and surreal experience for me, being surrounded by a dozen or so Catholics (the most in my lifetime in one space at a given time). It was the first time I had ever been up close to a Catholic priest let alone make small talk with him. The hostess of the meetings made me feel uncomfortable because she did not hesitate to share with me that she was once a Protestant but had became Catholic due to the importance of the sacraments and the richness of the theology in the Catholic Church. At first, she seemed rather pushy, doing apostolate on me! I was very content in my Protestant church and was not the least interested in anything else. (I should note that I came to love and admire this Catholic woman who would later become my first daughter's godmother). Tim continued to attend these meetings while in medical school, however I attended less frequently once I went on to teacher's college. It was through this group that we were befriending an increasing number of Catholics, something I did not necessarily intend to do. Nevertheless, I began to soften up to these new Catholic acquaintances and to accept that some Catholics are truly Christians, but perhaps they were only a minority.

We continued to attend the bible study at my home church but things started to get unpleasant. Tim's interpretation of Scripture was repeatedly at odds with the rest of the group. It became clearer that he was presenting Catholic interpretations of the passages we were studying. To make matters worse, there was a Catholic gentleman whom the leaders had invited to join the bible study (presumably in an attempt to rescue him from the Catholic Church) and he would often concur with what Tim was saying. This all made me feel uncomfortable and embarrassed. The other bible study group members were very respectful towards Tim and his comments, but I have no doubt they were probably praying hard that he would eventually come to see the truth.

As Tim continued to read and learn more about Catholicism, I became increasingly concerned and frustrated. I could not understand why he was so drawn to Catholicism because, to me, it seemed so contrary to biblical Christianity. As with other evangelicals who uphold the Protestant doctrine of sola scriptura (which incidentally was unheard of before the Reformation), I had always viewed the Bible as the only trustworthy source of God's Word and as having the final authority on matters of faith and morals – not the institutional church, not the pope – and so, for any article of faith to be true, it had to be in the Bible. Yet as I would find out later, this is not what the Bible itself says. *1 Timothy 3:15* says that the church is the "pillar and foundation of the truth", not Scripture. Indeed, Tim stated that both the written Word of God ('Sacred Scripture') and the oral teachings ('Sacred Tradition') of Jesus and His apostles together form the deposit of faith that has faithfully been handed down throughout the ages in the Catholic Church. Because Jesus condemned 'the traditions of men' (ex. *Mark 7:8, Matthew 15*), Protestants are often quick to view any teaching or practice not explicitly found in the Bible with suspicion. However, in *2 Thessalonians 2:15*, St. Paul urges believers to hold fast to and live according to the traditions, both written and oral, which have been handed down to them. In the New International Version of the Bible, the one used by many evangelicals, the word 'traditions' in 2 Thessalonians 2:15 has been changed to 'teachings', an example of their bias against 'tradition' (cf. *1 Corinthians 11:2, 2 Thessalonians 3:6*). Typically, *2 Timothy 3:16* is cited by evangelicals to defend the notion of sola scriptura and reaffirm the sufficiency of the Scriptures for guiding one's faith. But as Tim pointed out, this verse merely says "all" (and not "only") scripture is God-breathed and useful for teaching, correcting and training in righteousness, so that the man of God "may" (not "will") be thoroughly equipped for every good work. Also, nowhere in Scripture is *sola scriptura* taught. It was a classic example of circular reasoning. Furthermore, the Scripture referred to in *2 Timothy 3:16* is the Old Testament because the New Testament had not yet been written and compiled. There were many other instances where Protestants had let their preconceived notions cloud their understanding of what the Bible actually says.

When Tim informed me that Catholics believe that the Catholic Church is the one and the same church that Jesus Christ established over 2000 years ago founded on St. Peter, I was simply astounded at the arrogance and error of this claim. In my mind, I tried to rationalize it away thinking that, while on the surface it may appear to be a visible institution which dates back to the early Christians, in reality the true church which Christ intended was preserved by a faithful remnant of Christians who went underground at some point early on and then resurfaced after the Reformation, perhaps taking on various forms, yet in the end refined itself into the evangelical movement that we see today. This would account for the seemingly unadulterated, biblical version of Christianity of the evangelicals, who maintain that they share the same faith as the early Christians. While an interesting proposition, there was no empirical basis for this notion. I recall trying to articulate these ideas to Tim but was only met with frustration as he came back with proofs to the contrary. While he might have mentioned some scriptural support for the Catholic Church's claim (ex. Matthew 16:18-19), what I do remember were his constant references to the writings of the early Church Fathers. For me, though, this 'early Church' he was referring to was the yet unnamed Catholic Church, which had already deviated from the truth and had become corrupted by pagan influences. I did not believe that these so-called Church Fathers were teaching the authentic Christian faith as handed down by Jesus and His apostles. Yet, it never occurred to me that it was this same early Church was responsible for settling the canon of the Bible, in particular, which books would comprise the New Testament, the same New Testament used by Protestants. Nevertheless, I believed that the evangelical Protestants had the correct interpretation of Scripture and the Catholics did not.

Things went on like this for a while, with theological differences fuelling the tension growing between Tim and I. One big difference in opinion was that over the Eucharist which was so central to the Catholic faith. Firstly, the term 'Eucharist' was foreign to me, as was the idea of celebrating mass every day. In the church I grew up in, the Lord's Supper or Communion Service, as we called it, was celebrated only a few times a year. The rationale behind this infrequent occurrence was to make it more of a special event, and to avoid it becoming ritualistic (evangelicals have an aversion to anything ritualistic; vain rituals were for the pagans and were wholly condemned by Jesus). Secondly, in my church denomination, the Lord's Supper was considered a purely symbolic remembrance of Jesus' death rather than a sacrament as the Catholic Church understood it. Indeed, the idea of a sacrament as something that actually accomplishes what it signifies was also unbeknownst to me and seemed so outlandish. But when Tim laid out the vast Scriptural and historical support (enough evidence to fill an entire book) for the belief in the Eucharist as truly Jesus' Body and Blood, a belief held unequivocally by the early Christians (who recognized Jesus in 'the breaking of the bread', cf. *Luke 24:35, Acts 2:42*), I was absolutely stunned. It was a hard teaching for me, as it was for the disciples who abandoned Jesus after His discourse on the Bread of Life (*John 6:32-58*). How could the bread and wine received unworthily in *1 Corinthians 11:27-30* bring judgment upon oneself if they were only symbolic? If Catholics really believed that the Eucharist is truly Jesus, then it was no wonder why they bow down in worship and would want to receive the Eucharist as often as they could, even daily. Then I really became unsettled, for if all of this were true (which I wasn't willing to believe just yet), then how could this profound belief in the Real Presence of Christ in the Eucharist have not been taught or even mentioned in my Protestant upbringing? Was there anything else that I did not know of that the early Christians always believed which Protestants no longer believe? What else could I have been in the dark about? I was beginning to lose confidence in everything that I had been brought up to believe. It is hard to express how frightening it was to have the foundations for my faith start to crumble beneath me. It made me feel sick to my stomach.

I desperately needed to find ammunition to disprove the claims of Catholicism. I tried reading the Scriptural 'proof texts' that Tim was giving me but I was not convinced of the Catholic interpretations (which were often the most literal ones, especially in relation to the sacraments). I bought a Protestant study bible with commentaries written by various Protestant ministers, theologians, and authors. I was disappointed to find several unsatisfactory answers to some crucial questions. For example, one question was "Can someone who is saved fall away?" The answer provided was something like this: some say no because 'once saved, always saved' (another post-Reformation doctrine); some say yes, as several Scriptural passages attest to; and some say that if a person seriously falls away, then it means that they were never really saved in the first place (how then could anyone know for sure that they were saved, unless they were absolutely sure that they would never seriously fall away in the future?). There was hardly a consensus on every important issue, everything from baptism and communion as symbols or sacraments, to justification by faith alone or faith accompanied by works. Why was it that all these Christians, all guided by the same Holy Spirit, arrived at different interpretations? I was beginning to suspect what Tim had already suggested was true, that there was not one single doctrine in its entirety that all Protestants agreed upon and that while each Protestant denomination might arrive at some elements of the truth, the promise of the Holy Spirit to guide the church into the fullness of the truth (John 14:26, 16:13) was a gift given by Jesus to the Church founded on St. Peter, and not necessarily to all Christians. It was to this Church that Jesus promised that the gates of Hades shall not prevail over it (Matthew 16:19). In giving St. Peter the keys of the kingdom of heaven, Jesus was conferring primacy to St. Peter and his successors. Yet, given all this, I was still very sceptical of the authority of the Catholic Church, especially that of the pope.

An incident with our Bible study group echoed my sentiments of mistrust in the Catholic Church's claim of authority. When Tim was describing how Jesus founded His Church on St. Peter in Matthew 16:17-19, one of the members of the group was frantically ruffling through his Bible in disbelief to find the passage to see for himself. It is no wonder the passage had somehow escaped his attention in the past (as it had mine) because typically Protestant study bibles do not comment on this short yet significant passage (obviously in favour of the Catholic Church). The same fellow was baffled when the leader of the study group said he had read the Catechism of the Catholic Church and agreed with 90% of it. When asked why, if he agreed with most of it, he would not consider becoming Catholic, he responded "because of the hypocrisy in the Catholic Church". It is very unfortunate that the greatest stumbling block for many non-Catholics to discover the truth and beauty of the Catholic Church is the bad example of wayward Catholics. Despite all this, Jesus in Matthew 23:2-3 commanded the Hebrews to respect the authority of the Pharisees and do what they teach, but not what they do, for they sit on Moses' seat, the cathedra, which is a prefiguration of the seat of Peter.

Our squabbles about doctrine were to be set aside at least temporarily, for in 1996, Tim's mother grew ill with cancer. In a short few months, her condition had deteriorated to the point that surgery would be futile. Many prayers for healing were said by various Catholic, Protestant and Orthodox Christian friends and relatives. Tim's Catholic professor and the couple that hosted the Catholic Physicians' Guild meetings often visited and prayed for the intercession of then Blessed, now a canonized saint, St. Josemaria Escriva, the founder of Opus Dei. Although Tim's mother had not practised any faith for most of her life, she began to surrender her life into God's hands and her faith in Jesus grew tremendously in a short time. Tim's Orthodox sister arranged for their mother to see a priest and be anointed with holy oils from Jerusalem during holy week. She was extremely ill from sepsis and her body was shutting down. Then, amazingly, in the Triduum, the cancer seemed to miraculously have disappeared on the scans, much to the astonishment of her medical team. On Easter Sunday, she was deemed well enough to be sent home. I recall the wonderment as we all sat around the dinner table, celebrating a truly blessed and joyous Easter together. Sadly, the cancer returned and Tim's mother was re-hospitalized several weeks later. As she deteriorated rapidly, she knew of Tim's ardent interest in Catholicism and she eagerly wanted to embrace the Catholic faith as her own. She received a conditional baptism and entered the Church a few days before she died. Although Tim's family was devastated by her death, it had been a time of grace for them, for through these trials they had drawn closer together and closer to God, as each member had to confront the reality of death yet yearn for the hope of an afterlife. Tim's family and especially his mother had been greatly touched by the loving response of the various Catholic, Protestant and Orthodox Christians we knew, how they prayed for us and helped us in so many ways during that difficult year. It was a reminder that what separates us pales in comparison to the One who unites us as Christians.

Soon after Tim's mother died, Tim finally proposed to me, something I had been earnestly awaiting for several years. Now, however, came

144

another hurdle: we had to decide which church we would be married in. For me, it was a given – my home church, the one we had been attending together for the last couple of years. I knew that Tim yearned to become Catholic and that he probably desired to be married in the Catholic Church, but I would have none of that. Out of desperation, I was even open to considering the Orthodox Church, mostly because it was not Catholic. Indeed, we had experienced the beautiful liturgy at Tim's sister's Orthodox Church on a number of occasions and his sister seemed to be a wonderful Christian. Even though it had the same seven sacraments, Tim was dissatisfied with the lack of unity under one head and the lack of theological development in the Orthodox Church as compared to the Catholic Church. Because the Orthodox Church is divided among nationalistic lines, Tim thought it was not the catholic or 'universal' church that Jesus intended. So, we ended up being married in my Protestant church. Nearly all of those invited to our wedding were from my church. I was somehow hopeful that we were going to stay with that church for a long while.

Two months after we were married, I became pregnant with our first child. We knew virtually nothing about raising children. As Providence would have it, the Catholic lady who hosted the physicians' guild meetings encouraged us to take a certain parenting course run by some Catholics. Through attending this course, we became friends with several very sincere and faithful Catholics, who really knew their faith and again, surprisingly, their Bible. Furthermore, these Catholics lived out their faith with heroic virtue and I could truly see the light and love of Christ in them. But, as we were still attending my Protestant church, I made no mention of our new Catholic friends to our Protestant friends.

Meanwhile, Tim's interest in Catholicism had not waned as I had hoped. In fact, his study of Catholicism intensified during our first year of marriage. Because the majority of his ever-growing library of apologetics books seemed to emphasize a Catholic versus Protestant stance, I took this very personally. I felt insulted and betrayed. A great rift was growing between us and I cried out to God "Why are you doing this to us?" I had prayed that we would be united in our faith, but now it seemed otherwise. I became increasingly agitated when Tim would bring up the Catholic interpretation of Scriptural passages in our bible study group. It felt as though he was calling into question what I had always believed. It was much worse at home, for when the subject of Catholic beliefs was brought up at home, I would end up on the defensive and very angry on the inside. Eventually, I learned to change the subject and avoid conversations on religion altogether. But this avoidance strategy would be short-lived.

As the birth of our first baby was drawing ever near, the subject of infant baptism inevitably came up. In the church I grew up in, babies were generally not baptized and if they were baptized on extremely rare occasions, it was done as a symbolic gesture of dedication of an infant to the Lord rather than a sacrament that actually washes away sin and incorporates a person into the family of God. Despite my wishes to the contrary, I knew in my heart that our baby would end up being baptized Catholic because of Tim's growing conviction that infant baptism was important and necessary for our child. Although I did not want to hear it, Tim informed me that infant baptism was a practice that dated back to the early Church. What was even more astounding was that infant baptism actually had strong biblical support. Children were never excluded from the Old Covenant through circumcision, nor should they be excluded from the New Covenant through baptism in Jesus Christ (cf. *Col 2:11-12*). Just as all the Israelites were baptized in the Red Sea (1 Corinthians 10:2), in the New Testament, whole households were baptized (*Acts 16:15, 33; 18:8; 1 Corinthians 1:16*), which would certainly have included children and infants. Jesus Himself said in *Matthew 19:14 (Mark 10:14)* "Let the children come to me, and do not hinder them; for to such belongs the Kingdom of heaven." St. Peter exhorts in *Acts 2:38-39* "Repent and be baptized, every one of you…for this promise is for you and your children". Because God wishes all to be saved (*1 Timothy 2:4*) and because Scripture attests to the necessity of baptism (ex. *Matthew 28:19; Mark 16:16; John 3:5; Acts 22:16; Romans 6:3-5; 1 Corinthians 12:13; 1 Peter 3:2*), the Church baptizes infants. Baptism is a gift of God and the parents cooperate with God in initiating the child's spiritual life by baptizing their child in faith. If all this was true, I found it disturbing that my Protestant denomination and many others did not baptize infants as the early Christians did and always believed was necessary.

When our daughter Meghan was born, I was caught up with adjusting to life with a baby so I had little time to think about baptism. However, when Meghan was close to three months old, a concerned priest friend inquired when we were going to have her baptized. Rather than continue to resist, I eventually gave in, firstly, to avoid further conflict over the issue and, secondly, because I was not convinced that baptism accomplished anything anyway, I figured we would have nothing to lose. So, Meghan was baptized as a Catholic shortly after, with my Protestant family looking on with curiosity (and probably very uncomfortable being in a Catholic church, surrounded by Catholics making the sign of the cross, invoking the saints, etc.). Looking back, I always find it ironic yet at the same time beautiful that the youngest in our little family was the first to become a Catholic; she in a sense paved the way for the rest of us. (We also have no doubt that Tim's mother had something to do with it.)

In accepting to have Meghan baptized Catholic, as parents it was our responsibility to ensure that she would be raised in the Catholic faith, whether we became Catholic or not. (Although I at this point had absolutely no intention of becoming Catholic, I believe that Tim would have been Catholic by then if it were not for me holding him back.) For the sake of my daughter, I was open to checking out a local Catholic parish with Tim, one that we had heard good things about. It was to be my second or third time attending a Catholic mass. It was not at all what I was expecting. Quite opposite of being boring or lifeless, I was quite impressed by the congregation's zeal and the vibrant liturgy. In fact, the atmosphere was similar to what some evangelicals might be accustomed to. There was not a lot of mention of Mary or the saints, nor were there grand displays of statues (all of which were still stumbling blocks for me). There was a fair amount of Scripture reading and the homily was actually interesting. But the most important thing I noticed was that during the Mass, the emphasis was really on Christ Jesus, from beginning to end. I thought perhaps I could handle going to Mass with my daughter.

As part of my duty as a parent of a Catholic child to impart the Catholic faith and somewhat to satisfy my increasing curiosity, I started attending weekly doctrine classes at the local women's centre of Opus Dei. It is only by God's grace that I was even open to learning about the Catholic faith. At first, I found myself impressed by the richness and depth of Catholic theology, like nothing I had ever encountered before. The Catholic faith was both rational and mysterious. The woman who gave the doctrine classes was passionate about what she was teaching. I could see that theology, for her, was not only intellectually satisfying, it was an instrument that spiritually brought her closer to God. As the weeks progressed, to my great astonishment, the Catholic faith was starting to make sense to me! Furthermore, what I was hearing did not conflict with Scripture; on the contrary, Scripture seemed to support the various Catholic doctrines I was learning about. In fact, Catholic theology seemed to make more sense of Scripture. They seemed to go hand in hand. It was like I was uncovering a long-lost treasure. I found myself eager to learn more. Truth attracts, sometimes even the hardest of hearts.

Over the next few months, the Lord opened my eyes and my heart as I continued to learn more about Catholicism. I began reading testimonies of evangelical Protestants who became Catholic, very knowledgeable people, educated in theology, many of them ministers, people who struggled with the very same issues, who had dug deep into history and Scripture, and came to the surprising conclusion that they should become Catholic (as did John Henry Newman, an Anglican convert to Catholicism who said "To be deep in history is to cease being a Protestant.") I had heard of Catholics switching to Protestantism, but never this opposite phenomenon. Something was stirring in my heart and I had to admit that there must be some truth to what all these converts were saying given their plentiful evidence in support of their findings. In my pride, though, I was not going to let Tim know that he had perhaps been right all along about the Catholic Church. I kept all these insights to myself.

With more study, I was discovering that the Catholic Church was not at all the lost, unbiblical, man-made church I had initially thought. Historically, its lineage could indeed be traced back in unbroken continuity to the early church, the apostles, and Christ. I was impressed by the great unity of Catholics all over the world, unity in beliefs and in worship, in contrast to the thousands of different

Protestant denominations with so many different beliefs resulting from their reliance on the Bible alone. I came to understand how the Catholic Church is unified under one visible head and guided by the voice of Christ in His earthly representative, the Pope. I came to appreciate the importance of Sacred Tradition that together with Sacred Scripture imparted God's Word to Christians, a faith that has been transmitted faithfully down through the ages safeguarded by the teaching office of the Church, the Magisterium. Where I once thought of sacraments as unnecessary additions to the completed work of Jesus on the Cross, I came to understand the sacraments as graces flowing from Christ's redemption and as God's fatherly gifts to His Church, to be received, not earned. The sacraments were firmly rooted in Scripture and they dated back to the early Church, indeed instituted by Christ Himself. They were extensions of Christ's incarnation, physical means of channelling grace, life and power to Christians for every stage of their lives. I finally understood that honouring the saints does not detract anything from God, rather God their Creator is honoured and all the glory and praise goes back to their Father who raised them to be saints. The idea of praying to the saints no longer bothered me after I realized that when Catholics pray to the saints, they are asking for their intercession, much like we ask fellow Christians on earth for their prayers. I even found myself sometimes praying the Hail Mary in desperation while trying to soothe a crying baby in the middle of the night. Inevitably, I began to fall in love with the incredible beauty of the

Catholic faith, its doctrine and its liturgy, all of which were so imbued with Scripture. Yet, although the truth was staring me in the face, I was still too afraid to make the life-changing decision of converting to Catholicism and risk losing my friends, my family, my prestige. A lot was at stake and I was not willing to let my Protestant life go just yet.

It was the reading of one particular book, however, that was the major turning point for me. The book was Rome Sweet Home by Scott and Kimberley Hahn. I started reading it one day and I could not put it down. I very much identified with Kimberley's story of the struggles she and Scott experienced as he was being torn away from her as he drew closer to Catholicism and the agony she felt as he became Catholic while she and the rest of the family remained Protestant. But I was deeply moved to read of her incredible joy as she herself eventually came to embrace the Catholic faith and entered the Church. Upon finishing the book, it was as if the scales fell off my eyes: I was finally convinced of the historical authenticity of the Catholic Church and her God-given authority because Jesus Christ was her founder, and I firmly believed that she has in her the fullest expression of the Truth, in her doctrine, in her sacraments, in her liturgy, and especially in the blessed Fruit of her womb, Jesus, who is most truly and substantially present in the Eucharist. After putting my emotions aside and swallowing my pride, I finally admitted to Tim that I had been in the dark all these years but that now I was convinced we should become Catholic. I vividly remember the extraordinary release as I let go of all my stubbornness and bitterness that had been festering in my soul for the last few months. Tears and embracing ensued and my heart flooded with indescribable joy, for now we could both proceed, finally, united in faith towards our true homeland where God had called us. As I look back, I am so grateful that, despite my resistance, Tim never gave up hope as he patiently let the Holy Spirit work in me to bring me home. Tim had so longed for both of us to come home to the Catholic Church, and now that we were on the threshold, he was over-joyed and praised God for His infinite goodness.

Tim and I took a fast-track RCIA course and we were on our way to be received into the Catholic Church at the upcoming Easter Vigil. In preparation, I was first required to go to the Sacrament of Confession. The idea of confession to a priest was so foreign to me, especially after years of a me-and-Jesus-only relationship, confessing directly to God in private. Furthermore, I had never even been in a confessional before. I was actually quite terrified at the prospect of laying out a lifetime's worth of sins to another human being. But firmly believing that the priest was representing Christ in confession, my first confession was an unforgettable experience. God's grace flooded my soul and washed it clean, filling it with joy. I had never felt completely for-given until then. Moreover, I felt God's grace em-powering me to begin anew.

It was Easter Vigil, April 3, 1999. The time had finally come for us to be received into the Catholic Church, I, by the Sacrament of Confirmation, and Tim, by the Sacraments of Baptism and Confirmation.

With Tim's graduate studies professor standing by his side as his godfather, and my good friend standing by my side as my sponsor, we entered the glorious Church. I sensed all of heaven was celebrating the homecoming of these two souls. Tim's godfather remarked that "someone in heaven must be very happy today", referring to Tim's mother who we now have no doubt had been interceding for us to become Catholic, but also surely our Mother Mary was there to receive us with wide open arms of love. In partaking of our First Communion, we indeed were able to 'taste and see that the Lord is good'. I was overwhelmed with such profound peace, and my heart sang out the beloved melody from my childhood "It is well with my soul."

In the weeks to follow, we had the painful task of informing our evangelical friends that we had become Catholic. They had no idea we had been contemplating such a thing, because we had continued to attend my old church while preparing to be received into the Catholic Church. Needless to say, their response to our big news was one of utter shock and disbelief. Some were very angry and disappointed, especially those from our Bible study group, those whom we learned, shared and prayed with, and had come to love and deeply respect. Others politely said they were happy that we had found unity in faith as a couple and wished us well. But, in reality, most of our friends must have felt betrayed and very sorry for us that we had, in their minds, lost our way. We even shared some of the reasons why we became Catholic, providing historical and Scriptural support behind our decisions, but all this was to no avail. Within a short time, as we were attending Catholic mass every Sunday instead of services in my old church, and since we lived across town, but most likely because they did not want to have anything to do with us, our evangelical friends sadly faded from our lives. It was the bittersweet end of one chapter in our lives, but the beginning of yet another, more glorious one. We were embarking on a grand new adventure, albeit without our beloved friends.

Our new life in the Catholic Church was marked with the joy of a new springtime. We found ourselves heartily welcomed into a vibrant local parish. In no time, we became involved in parish life and made many wonderful Catholic friends. With a renewed openness to life and the Holy Spirit, our family blossomed, as one after another, our children were born and by God's grace received the extraordinary heritage of divine sonship and incorporation into the Catholic Church through their baptism. In His great goodness, God blessed us with on-going spiritual formation and friendships in Opus Dei. Indeed, we would not be Catholic today if God had not placed these wonderful, devout Catholics in our paths. We are truly thankful for the tremendous support and prayers of these friends and the many other splendid Catholics we have met along the way who continue to inspire us as they live out their vocations with saintly fortitude.

It is with wonder and thanksgiving that I look back at the abundant graces God has showered upon me, as He drew me ever nearer to His fold and my home in the Catholic Church, even from my

Protestant beginnings. I am truly grateful for my Protestant upbringing, which initiated me in my Christian walk, helped me to nurture a personal relationship with Christ, instilled in me a profound respect for Scripture, and taught me the meaning of discipleship. I thank God for the grace of a Christian home. I will always cherish the quiet, loving example that my mother always provided, and her steadfast devotion to Jesus, like His own Mother had toward Him. I will also treasure the loving support and prayers of my sister and brother, who respected me and considered me a fellow Christian even as I became Catholic. There are so many wonderful Protestant Christians as there are Catholic Christians yet both have much to learn from each other. It is my earnest prayer that God would heal the wounds of division among the Christian churches, and one day gather them all to Himself as one fold.

> The moment men cease to pull against [the Catholic Church] they feel a tug towards it. The moment they cease to shout it down they begin to listen to it with pleasure. The moment they try to be fair to it they begin to be fond of it. But when that affection has passed a certain point it begins to take on the tragic and menacing grandeur of a great love affair... When he has entered the Church, he finds that the Church is much larger inside than it is outside." – G. K. Chesterton, *The Catholic Church and Conversion*

This Easter marks the tenth anniversary of our entering the Catholic Church. While, like Abraham relocating to a foreign land, we have left much behind, losing friends and respect along the way, there have been absolutely no regrets and we are confident that God has led us to our true home. As with stained glass, when one looks at the Church from the outside, it initially appears dark, somewhat dreary and rather indistinct. But once inside, its magnificence is revealed as the Son Light shines through and illuminates its wonderfully grand design and purpose. Now that we are on the inside, we never cease to be amazed at the inexhaustible treasures to be found.

In the Church, we have found a pearl of great price, more valuable than all the riches of this world, worth giving up everything to possess – that is, Our Lord Jesus in the Blessed Sacrament. It is the greatest mystery that Our Lord Jesus chooses to unite Himself to His people in the most intimate and humble manner in the Eucharist, and He stays with us, lovingly waiting for us in the Tabernacle of every Catholic Church. From the Eucharist, all of the other sacraments flow. Knowing that we would need all the help we could get on our earthly pilgrimage towards heaven, Jesus left us the Church and the sacraments as gifts out of His tremendous love for us.

In the Church, we are blessed with a family we never knew, a family more vast and marvellous than we ever dreamed of. We now behold the blessed Mother Mary as our spiritual mother, who loves us with a mother's heart, most powerfully intercedes for us, and shows us how to get closer to her Son. In addition to fellow Christians in the Church Militant and Church Suffering, we also have countless holy siblings, those crowned brothers and sisters in heaven, who surround us as a great cloud of witnesses, cheering us on as we struggle on our way to the finish line. What a great privilege it is to share in a spiritual solidarity with the saints, in whom God's glory and handiwork are splendidly revealed. In His great love and wisdom, God has graciously given us a Holy Father to unite His family and to shepherd His flock on earth. Through the popes, we have heard the voice of Christ throughout the ages. It gives us great reassurance knowing that we stand on the shoulders of giants. The Catholic Church has stood firm for over two millennia, with unwavering faith, even in the face of trials and persecutions, remaining steadfast in defending the truth without compromise.

For our family, our journey has just begun. Each day is part of an ongoing unveiling of the glorious splendour and fullness of the Church. What we experience is only a pale shadow of what is to be revealed in all its grandeur in the age to come. It is my ardent prayer that my family, now and in the generations to come, and Catholics everywhere will ever more grow in love with Jesus and His one, holy, catholic and apostolic Church, and always cherish and remain close to their mother Church, forever under the mantle of their Blessed Mother Mary.

# Richard John Neuhaus

**Richard John Neuhaus was born in Pembroke, Ontario. He was an ordained Lutheran priest. He is the author of *The Naked Public Square* and *Death on a Friday Afternoon*. He is founder and first editor of *First Things*, an influential journal of religion, culture and public affairs. He died in January, 2009. (This essay was published in the April 2002 issue of *First Things*.)**

## How I Became the Catholic I Was

This is more a story than an argument. It is in some ways a very personal story, and yet not without broader implications. It is just possible that some may discern in the story suggestions of an argument, even an argument about the nature of Lutheranism, and of Protestantism more generally.

When in 1990 I was received by the late John Cardinal O'Connor into full communion with the Catholic Church – on September 8, the Nativity of Our Lady – I issued a short statement in response to the question Why. With Lutheran friends especially in mind, I said, "To those of you with whom I have traveled in the past, know that we travel together still. In the mystery of Christ and his Church nothing is lost, and the broken will be mended. If, as I am persuaded, my communion with Christ's Church is now the fuller, then it follows that my unity with all who are in Christ is now the stronger. We travel together still."

When Cardinal Newman was asked at a dinner party why he became a Catholic, he responded that it was not the kind of thing that can be properly explained between soup and the fish course. When asked the same question, and of course one is asked it with great frequency, I usually refer to Newman's response. But then I add what I call the short answer, which is simply this: I became a Catholic in order to be more fully what I was and who I was as a Lutheran. The story that follows may shed some light on that short answer.

In the statement of September 8, 1990, I also said:

> I cannot express adequately my gratitude for all the goodness I have known in the Lutheran communion. There I was baptized, there I learned my prayers, there I was introduced to Scripture and creed, there I was nurtured by Christ on Christ, there I came to know the utterly gratuitous love of God by which we live astonished. For my theological formation, for friendships beyond numbering, for great battles fought, for mutual consolations in defeat, for companionship in ministry – for all this I give thanks... As for my thirty years as a Lutheran pastor, there is nothing in that ministry that I would repudiate, except my many sins and shortcomings. My becoming a priest in the Roman Catholic Church will be the completion and right ordering of what was begun all those years ago. Nothing that is good is rejected, all is fulfilled.

Begin at St. John's Lutheran Church in the Ottawa Valley of Canada. To be brought up a

Lutheran, at least a Missouri Synod Lutheran, at least there and at least then, was to know oneself as an ecclesial Christian. Of course I did not put it that way as a young boy, nor was it put that way to me, but I would later see what had happened. An ecclesial Christian is one who understands with mind and heart, and even feels with his fingertips, that Christ and his Church, head and body, are inseparable. For the ecclesial Christian, the act of faith in Christ and the act of faith in the Church are not two acts of faith but one. In the words of the third century St. Cyprian, martyr bishop of Carthage, "He who would have God as his Father must have the Church as his mother." In an important sense, every Christian, even the most individualistic, is an ecclesial Christian, since no one knows the gospel except from the Church. *Extra ecclesiam nulla salus* – no salvation outside the Church – applies to all. For some, that truth is incidental; for the ecclesial Christian it is constitutive, it is at the very core, of faith and life.

In my Missouri Synod childhood there were seemingly little things that made a big difference. Some would call them "nontheological factors," but I see now that they were fraught with theological significance. Across the street from the parsonage of St. John's was an evangelical Protestant church. Also across the street lived my best friends, the Spooner brothers, who with their devoutly Catholic family attended St. Columkil's Cathedral. I am sure it was unarticulated but self-evident to me by the time I was five years old that St. John's and the cathedral had more in common than either had with the evangelical chapel. For one immeasurably momentous thing, our churches baptized babies. Then too, our being saved was something that God did through His Church; it was a given, a gift. It did not depend – as it did for Dougy Cahill, our evangelical friend – upon feelings or spiritual experience. It depended upon grace bestowed through things done.

Unlike the Spooner boys, I was in catechism class taught to speak of sola gratia, and was told that the truth in that phrase divided us from the Catholics, but, as best I can remember, I was much more impressed by the gratia and disinclined to pick a fight over the sola. We both knew that we were to keep the commandments and try to please God in all that we did. The distinction supposedly was that I, as a Lutheran, tried to be good in gratitude for being saved, while Catholics tried to be good in order to be saved. I don't recall ever discussing this with the Spooner boys, but I expect we would have thought it a distinction without much of a difference. We knew we were baptized children of God for whom Christ died, and that it was a very bad thing to get on God's wrong side. In catechism class I was told that they, as Catholics, were more afraid of God's punishment than I, who was sure of forgiveness, but I never noticed that to be the case.

Don't get me wrong. I was not theologically precocious at age five, or even ten. I was not even especially devout. I really didn't like having to go to church. But I am looking back now, trying to understand the formation of an ecclesial Christian – a Christian of lower-case catholic sensibilities who

162

would, step by step, be led to upper-case Catholic allegiance. There were other seemingly little things. St. John's and the other Lutheran churches I knew had a high altar. As did the cathedral. With candles. Also important, there was not a bare cross but a crucifix. And a communion rail at which we knelt and received what we were taught was really and truly and without any equivocation the Body and Blood of Christ. As were the Spooner boys taught, and as we both said we believed although we agreed that we sure couldn't figure it out. And we had catechisms to memorize that were almost identical in format and questions, although not always in answers. And everybody knew that the way to tell the difference between Catholic and Lutheran churches and all the others is that Catholics and Lutherans put a cross on top of their steeples instead of a weather vane or nothing at all.

Then too, although in catechism class I heard about sola scriptura, we both knew we had a Magisterium, although I'm sure I never heard the term. When it came to settling a question in dispute, they had the pope – and we had the faculty of Concordia Seminary in St. Louis. It was perfectly natural to ask the question, "What's our position on this or that?" The "our" in the question self-evidently referred to the Missouri Synod, and the answer was commonly given by reference to an article in the synod's official publication, The Lutheran Witness, usually written, or so it seemed, by Dr. Theodore Graebner. Why the Spooners went to one church and we to another seemed obvious enough; they were Catholics and we were Lutherans. They were taught that they belonged to the "one true Church" and I was taught that I belonged to the Missouri Synod and all those who are in doctrinal agreement with the Missouri Synod, which community made up "the true visible Church on earth." So, between their ecclesiological claim and ours, it seemed pretty much a toss-up. They were taught that, despite my not belonging to the one true Church, I could be saved by virtue of "invincible ignorance." I was taught that, despite their not belonging to the true visible Church on earth, they could be saved by – in the delicious phrase of Francis Pieper, Missouri's chief dogmatician – "felicitous inconsistency."

I doubt if ever for a moment the Spooner boys thought that maybe they should be Lutheran. I am sure that I as a boy thought – not very seriously, certainly not obsessively – but I thought about being a Catholic. It seemed that, of all the good things we had, they had more. Catholicism was more. Then too, I knew where all those good things we had came from. They came from the church that had more. Much later I would hear the schism of the sixteenth century described as, in the fine phrase of Jaroslav Pelikan, a "tragic necessity." I thought, then and now, that the tragedy was much more believable than the necessity. But in my boyhood, the division did not seem tragic. It was just the way things were. I do not recall anything that could aptly be described as anti-Catholicism. My father's deer hunting buddy was a Catholic priest, and deer hunting, for my Dad, was something very close to *communicatio in sacris*. In the Missouri Synod of those days, praying with Catholics – or anyone else with whom we were not in complete doctrinal agreement – was condemned as "unionism." The rules didn't say anything about the deep communion of deer hunting.

Of course, we kids went to different schools; they to the "separate" (meaning Catholic) school and we to the "public" (meaning Protestant) school. Sometimes they would walk home on one side of the street and shout, "Catholic, Catholic ring the bell / Protestant, Protestant go to hell." To which we on the other side of the street reciprocated by reversing the jingle. It was all in good fun, much like a school cheer. I don't think for a moment that either of us thought it had any reference to the other's eternal destiny. It is just the way things were. There were other differences. Tommy and Eddie went to confession, and I was curious about that. At St. John's Lutheran, on Saturday evenings before "communion Sunday," people came to "announce" for communion, a pale ritual trace of what had once been confession, utterly devoid of any sense of sacramental mystery. It was a simple matter of writing down their names in the "communion book," and, if my Dad wasn't there to do it, it was done by my mother or one of my older siblings.

And there was this: St. Columkil's had a bishop, put there, it was said, by the pope in Rome. St. John's had, well, my Dad, put there, as he told the story, by his seminary classmate who got him the call. To be sure it was, in Missouri parlance, a "divine call," but I wonder now if as a child I intuited that there was, between Bishop Smith and my Dad, some qualitative difference of ecclesial authority. Not that I was inclined to doubt what my Dad taught. After all, he had the Bible, Martin Luther, and the St. Louis faculty on his side. And he was indisputably authoritative in manner. Not for nothing during his days at seminary was he called "Pope Neuhaus." But this young boy sensed, although he could not say just how, that between the Bishop of Pembroke and the pastor of St. John's Lutheran Church in Pembroke, there was a qualitative difference of office.

It was not a matter of life-or-death urgency. Live and let live was the order of the day. Where we differed, we were right and they were wrong. In disagreeing with Catholics, everybody on our side – what was vaguely described as the Protestant side – was agreed. But then, we Lutherans disagreed with many Protestants and took the Catholic side when it came to, for instance, baptizing babies and knowing that Jesus is really and truly and without equivocation present in the Holy Communion. It was all very confusing, and didn't bear too much thinking about. I would in time come to understand that the question is that of authority, and it must be thought about very carefully indeed.

I will return to the question of authority, but for now I simply underscore the ways in which being brought up a Missouri Lutheran – at least then and at least there – produced an ecclesial Christian. One might also speak of a sacramental Christian or an incarnational Christian, but, whatever the terminology, the deepest-down conviction, the most irrepressible sensibility, is that of the touchability, the visibility, the palpability of what we might call "the Christian thing." To use the language of old eucharistic controversies, *finitum capax infiniti* – the finite is capable of the infinite. Put differently, there is no access to the infinite except through the finite. Or yet again, God's investment in the finite can be trusted infinitely. Although Lutheran theology discarded the phrase, it is the *ex opere operato* conviction evident in Luther's ultimate defiance of Satan's every temptation by playing the trump card, "I am baptized!" *Ex opere operato* is the sacramental enactment of sola gratia. It is uncompromisingly objective. By it morbid introspection, the delusions of religious enthusiasm, and the endlessly clever postulations of the theological imagination are called to order by truth that is answerable to no higher truth; for it is Christ, who is the Truth, who speaks in the voice of his Church – "I baptize you..." "I forgive you your sins..." "This is my body..."

Moving forward to my teenage years, I had in high school what our evangelical friends would call a born-again experience, and for a time viewed with contempt the ritual and sacramental formalities of what I thought to be a spiritually comatose Lutheranism. For a time, I suppose I might have been a good candidate for the Baptist ministry, but it did not last. Missouri's traditional hostility toward "pietism" – an exaggerated emphasis on the affective dimension of Christian faith – struck me as hostility toward piety. But after a period of frequently anguished uncertainty about the possibility of sorting out subjective experience and egotistic assertiveness from the workings of grace, I came to a new appreciation of Luther's warnings against religious enthusiasm. Several years later, at Concordia, St. Louis, I was to discover the possible synthesis of piety, clear reason, and ecclesial authority in the person and teaching of Professor Arthur Carl Piepkorn.

The students most closely gathered around him called him – behind his back, to be sure – "the Pieps," and those who in American Lutheranism today describe themselves as "Evangelical Catholics" – perhaps a fourth or more of the clergy – are aptly called the Piepkornians. Piepkorn was a man of disciplined prayer and profound erudition, and was deeply engaged in the liturgical renewal and the beginnings of Lutheran–Roman Catholic dialogue. At St. Louis he taught the Lutheran confessional writings of the sixteenth century, which he insistently called "the symbolical books of the Church of the Augsburg Confession." They were, he insisted, the "symbols" of a distinctive communion within the communion of the one, holy, catholic, and apostolic Church. They represented a way of being catholic as the heirs of a Reformation that was intended to be a movement of reform within and for the one Church of Christ.

Piepkorn underscored the Church's tradition prior to the Reformation, the tradition of which Lutheranism was part. The accent was on continuity, not discontinuity. Perhaps the sixteenth century break was necessary – although that was never emphasized – but certainly the Lutheran Reformation, unlike other movements that claimed the

Reformation heritage, had no delusions about being a new beginning, a so-called rediscovery of the gospel, by which the authentic and apostolic Church was reconstituted. Lutheranism was not a new beginning but another chapter in the history of the one Church. The Church is not a theological school of thought, or a society formed by allegiance to theological formulas – not even formulas such as "justification by faith" – but is, rather, the historically specifiable community of ordered discipleship through time, until the end of time. Piepkorn emphasized that we are Christians first, catholic Christians second, and Lutheran Christians third. In this understanding, the goal was to fulfill the promise of the Lutheran Reformation by bringing its gifts into full communion with the Great Tradition that is most fully and rightly ordered through time in the Roman Catholic Church.

In this understanding, the conclusion of the Augsburg Confession of 1530 was taken to be normative. There the signers declare:

> Only those things have been recounted which it seemed necessary to say in order that it may be understood that nothing has been received among us, in doctrine or in ceremonies, that is contrary to Scripture or to the Church catholic. For it is manifest that we have guarded diligently against the introduction into our churches of any new and ungodly doctrines.

For us Piepkornians, everything was to be held accountable to that claim. In some streams of Lutheran orthodoxy, as well as in Protestant liberalism, a very different notion of normatively was proposed. In the language of the twentieth-century Paul

169

Tillich, catholic substance was to be held in tension with Protestant principle, with Protestant principle having the corrective and final word. But a principle that is not part of the substance inevitably undermines the substance. And what is called the Protestant principle is, as we know from sad experience, so protean, so subject to variation, that it results either in the vitiation of doctrine itself or further schism in the defence of doctrinal novelty. Theology that is not in service to "the faith once delivered to the saints" (*Jude 3*) turns against the faith once delivered to the saints. Ideas that are not held accountable to "the Church of the living God, the pillar and bulwark of truth" (*1 Timothy 3:15*) will in time become the enemy of that truth. Such was our understanding of the normative claim of the Augustana to have received nothing contrary to Scripture or to the Catholic Church.

But the Lutheran chapter in the history of the Church did occasion schism, and for that unhappy fact there was blame enough to share all around. In my judgment, the division was tragic but not necessary. There was and is no truth that requires division from the pillar and bulwark of truth. The Catholic Church, as Chesterton observed, is ever so much larger from the inside than from the outside. And especially is that the case, I would add, for those whose identity as Protestants depends upon their being outside. And so it was that for thirty years as a Lutheran pastor, thinker, and writer, as editor of *Una Sancta*, an ecumenical journal of theology, and, later, Forum Letter, an independent Lutheran publication, I worked for what I incessantly called "the healing of the breach of the sixteenth century between Rome and the Reformation." For a long time there seemed to be believable, albeit painfully slow, movement toward that goal. Very hopeful was the reappropriation of the Lutheran tradition associated with the nineteenth-century "evangelical catholic," Wilhelm Loehe, and the ressourcement – the going back to the sources – evident in the 1970s production and reception of the Lutheran Book of Worship. Then too, there were promising new levels of understanding and theological reconciliation achieved in the formal Lutheran-Roman Catholic theological dialogues. These hopeful signs, however, were not to last.

The last several decades have not been kind to Lutheranism. By the end of the 1980s it seemed evident to me that real, existent Lutheranism – as distinct from Lutheranism as an idea or school of thought – had, willy-nilly but decisively, turned against the fulfillment of its destiny as a reforming movement within the one Church of Christ. Lutheranism in all its parts, both in this country and elsewhere, had settled for being a permanently separated Protestant denomination; or, as the case may be, several Protestant denominations. Some of my Lutheran friends say that, in entering into full communion with the Catholic Church, I acted precipitously, I jumped the gun. To which I say that I hope they are right; and if, someday in some way that cannot now be foreseen, there is ecclesial reconciliation and a healing of the breach of the sixteenth century, I hope that my decision will have played at least a minuscule part in that happy outcome.

Mine was a decision mandated by conscience. I have never found it in his writings, but a St. Louis professor who had been his student told me that the great confessional Lutheran theologian Peter Brunner regularly said that a Lutheran who does not daily ask himself why he is not a Roman Catholic cannot know why he is a Lutheran. That impressed me very deeply. I was thirty years a Lutheran pastor, and after thirty years of asking myself why I was not a Roman Catholic I finally ran out of answers that were convincing either to me or to others. And so I discovered not so much that I had made the decision as that the decision was made, and I have never looked back, except to trace the marks of grace, of sola gratia, each step of the way.

My reception occasioned some little comment, including the observation that I and others who make this decision have a "felt need for authority." This is usually said in a condescending manner by people who believe that they are able to live with ambiguities and tensions that some of us cannot handle. Do I have a felt need for authority, for obedience, for submission? But of course. Obedience is the rightly ordered disposition toward truth, and submission is subordination of the self to that by which the self is claimed. Truth commands, and authority has to do with the authorship, the origins, of commanding truth. By what authority? By whose authority? There are no more important questions for the right ordering of our lives and ministries. Otherwise, in our preaching, teaching, and entire ministry we are just making it up as we go along, and, by acting in God's name, taking His name in vain.

It was sadly amusing to read that a Lutheran denomination in this country is undertaking a major study with a view toward revising its teaching on sexual morality, with particular reference to homosexuality. Especially striking was the assurance that the study would be conducted "without any prior assumptions." Imagine that. The entire course of Christian fidelity is obedience to the received truth of God's self-revelation in Jesus Christ, and the Spirit's guiding of the Church's reflection on that truth. At some point this Lutheran body will arrive at its new teaching. Through a complicated process of bureaucratic planning, interest group agitation, and a legitimating majority vote, it will eventually arrive at the point of saying "this we believe, teach, and confess." Undoubtedly Scripture will be cited, but, as Luther said, biblical texts, like wax noses, can be twisted to fit. If, as seems probable, this body adopts a new teaching and one asks by what authority it teaches this new doctrine, the only honest answer will be, "Because we will it to be so." "It is what was decided by the procedures adopted by our religious society," they might say. "Ours is, after all, a voluntary association, so nobody else has any right to complain." By the rules of that denomination, the Church through time and the contemporary Church universal, to which Christ promised the Spirit's guidance, does not get a vote.

From my boyhood intuitions as an ecclesial Christian, it seemed self-evident that, if God intended to reveal any definite truths for the benefit of humankind, and if Jesus intended a continuing community of discipleship, then some reliable means would be provided for the preservation and transmission of such truths through the centuries. Catholics believe that God did provide such reliable means by giving the apostles and their successors, the bishops, authority to teach in His name and by promising to be with them forever. The teaching of the apostles and of the apostolic churches, securely grounded in the biblical Word of God, continues to this day, and will continue to the end of time. Catholics believe that, under certain carefully prescribed circumstances, the pope and the whole body of bishops are able to teach with infallibility. That is a word that frightens many, but I don't think it should. It means that the Church is indefectible, that we have God's promise that He will never allow the Church to definitively defect from the truth, to fall into apostasy. Infallibility, Avery Cardinal Dulles writes, "is simply another way of saying that the Holy Spirit will preserve the Church against using its full authority to require its members to assent to what is false." Without that assurance, he adds, "the truth of revelation would not be preserved in recognizable form." And, I would add, to obey the truth we must be able to recognize the truth.

The question of authority, the question of Who says so?, has been with the Church from the beginning. In Corinth some invoked Peter, some Paul, some Apollos, and some Christ. And so it was later with the Montanists, the Arians, the Nestorians, the Valentinians, the Donatists, and on and on. A sure mark of a heretical and schismatic community, said St. Augustine, is that it names itself by a man or an idea rather than by the simple title "Catholic." Also centuries later, for example in the sixteenth century, those who had sense enough to know that the Church did not begin with their new theological insight tried to reconstruct Christian history to fit their views. Thus the Lutheran Matthias Illyricus Flacius compiled the Magdeburg Centuries; thus followers of John Knox claimed to have reestablished the polity of the New Testament Church; thus the "Landmarkist" historiography of American Baptists who trace the lineage of the one true Church through Cathari, Waldensians, Lollards, Albigenses, and all the way back to Jesus himself. All such efforts attempt to answer the question of authority. Some are less ludicrous than others, but none is plausible. As St. Augustine and all Catholic teachers have known, the teaching of the Church is lived forward, not reconstructed backward.

St. Augustine appealed to the *securus judicat orbis terrarum* – the secure judgment of the whole world, by which he meant the Catholic Church. Yes, but what do you do when that judgment is unclear or in heated dispute? Augustine's answer is that you wait, in firm communion with the Catholic Church and in firm confidence that the Holy Spirit will, as promised, clarify the matter in due course. The point is that apostolic doctrine cannot be maintained over time without apostolic ministry, meaning ministry that is both apostolic in its origins and apostolic in its governing authority. This argument is brilliantly advanced in his polemic against the Donatists, who appealed to St. Cyprian as precedent for refusing to recognize the sacraments of the *traditores*, those who had lapsed in time of persecution.

Yes, answered Augustine, the holy Cyprian was confused, and admitted as much; but he awaited clarification by the *securus judicat orbis terrarum*. The one thing he would not do, unlike the Donatists, was to break communion with the Catholic Church.

The Church is holy in practice and correct in doctrine, said the schismatic Donatists, and therefore it cannot exist in communion with the unholy and erring. It follows that the Donatists are the true Church. To which Augustine replied:

> If, therefore, by such communion with the wicked the just cannot but perish, the Church had already perished in the time of Cyprian. Whence then sprang the origin of Donatus? Where was he taught, where was he baptized, where was he ordained, since [you claim that] the Church had been already destroyed by the contagion of communion with the wicked? But if the Church still existed, the wicked could do no harm to the good in one communion with them. Wherefore did you separate yourselves?

"Wherefore did you separate yourselves?" Augustine's question echoes down through the centuries, directed at all who have separated themselves from communion with the Catholic Church. Today the criticism is heard that the Catholic Church, for all its magisterial authority, will permit almost anything in teaching or practice so long as one does not formally break communion with the Church. There is truth in that, although I think it not a criticism but a compliment. While what Lutherans call the *publica doctrina*, the public teaching, of the Catholic Church is lucidly clear, it is true that the Church bends every effort, puts the best construction on every deviant opinion, in order to avoid what Augustine calls "the heinous and damnable sin of schism." For instance, in the twenty-three years of the supposedly authoritarian pontificate of John Paul II, the number of theologians publicly censured can probably be counted on the fingers of one hand, and the only schism has been that of the integrist Lefebvrists of France. Disagreement, confusion, and false teaching can do great evil, but the remedy for such evil is always to be found in communion with that body that is gifted with the charism of providing *securus judicat orbis terrarum*.

Councils can err, said the Reformers. No, says the Catholic Church, but the Church's teaching lives forward, and no definition, including that of councils, is entirely adequate to the whole of the truth. The Catholic Church has always taught with St. Paul that now, as he says in 1 Corinthians 13, we see in a mirror dimly, but then face to face. Now we know in part; then we shall understand fully, even as we have been fully understood. Along the way to that eschatological fullness – which is a frequently jagged, confusing, and conflicted way – it is promised to the Church that she will not, she will not irretrievably, lose the way. It is not everything that we might want, but it is enough; it is more than enough.

The Church's teaching lives forward; it is not reconstructed backward – whether from the fifth century or the sixteenth or the nineteenth or the twenty-first. But through all the changes of living forward, how do we know what is corruption and what is authentic development? Recall Cardinal

Newman's reflection on the development of doctrine, a reflection that has been incorporated by magisterial teaching. He suggested seven marks of authentic development: Authentic development preserves the Church's apostolic form; it reflects continuity of principles in testing the unknown by the known; it demonstrates the power to assimilate what is true, even in what is posited against it; it follows a logical sequence; it anticipates future developments; it conserves past developments; and, throughout, it claims and demonstrates the vigour of teaching authority. And thus it is, said St. Vincent of Lerins in the fifth century, that in authentic development of doctrine nothing presents itself in the Church's old age that was not latent in her youth. Such was the truth discovered by Augustine, a truth "ever ancient, ever new."

And so it is that this ecclesial Christian, this son of St. John's Lutheran Church in Pembroke, this former Lutheran pastor of St. John the Evangelist in Brooklyn, was led to September 8, 1990, to be received into full communion by John Cardinal O'Connor in his residence chapel of St. John the Evangelist, my patron saint. In every way, including my awareness of the intercession of St. John, the continuities are ever so much more striking than the discontinuities. In the words of the Second Vatican Council, my Protestant brothers and sisters are, by virtue of baptism and faith in Christ, truly but imperfectly in communion with the Catholic Church. Which means also, of course, that I am truly but imperfectly in communion with them. Moreover, and according to the same Council, all the saving and sanctifying grace to be found outside the boundaries of the Catholic Church gravitates toward the perfection of that imperfect communion. Some view the Catholic Church as claiming to be self-sufficient, but that is not true. Her ecclesiology is such that, of all Christian communions, she knows herself to be most in need. Nowhere are the words *Ut unum sint*, "that they may all be one," prayed so fervently; nowhere is the wound of our broken communion felt so keenly; nowhere is the commitment to reconciliation so relentless or irrevocable.

It would take another essay to survey the current prospect for such reconciliation. Suffice it to say that, whether with respect to the Orthodox Church of the East or the separated communions of the West, these are hard times for ecumenism, hard times for the hope for Christian unity. But the Church has known many times that were harder, much harder; she has learned that the better part of fidelity is sometimes simply persistent waiting upon the movement of the Holy Spirit toward possibilities that she can neither anticipate nor control, but for which we must together pray.

As for now, I end where I began – as in my life's course I began where I have ended – by saying again: "To those of you with whom I have traveled in the past, know that we travel together still. In the mystery of Christ and his Church nothing is lost, and the broken will be mended. If, as I am persuaded, my communion with Christ's Church is now the fuller, then it follows that my unity with all who are in Christ is now the stronger. We travel together still."

179

# Eric Nicolai

**Eric Nicolai was born in Montreal in 1963 of German immigrants of Lutheran background. His family moved to Oakville in 1983. He began his university studies in Toronto, went on to get a B.A. in art history at McGill University and completed an M.A. in art history at the Université Laval in Quebec City in 1990. In September 1990, he began studies in theology at the Pontifical University of the Holy Cross in Rome, and in 1994 was ordained to the priesthood for the Prelature of Opus Dei. He completed his doctorate in theology in 1995. He is currently chaplain of Riverview Centre in Montreal, Canada.**

## Country Road, Take Me Home

My parents arrived in Montreal in 1962 from Hamburg, Germany. My father had worked in Hamburg for an international freight forwarding firm and was offered a post in the new Montreal branch. The only contact I ever had with any church growing up was the occasional Sunday service at a Lutheran parish in St. Lambert, a well-established neighbourhood on the South Shore of Montreal. It was very small and my

180

memories of these visits are vague. My parents told me that it was mainly a way to get to know people, and visits to this small community did not continue for very long. I remember that the church building was sold a few years later and converted into a regular suburban family dwelling. That was similar to what happened to religion in our home: It started as a curiosity and eventually dissipated into everyday life.

My sister and I enrolled in the French immersion program at an English Protestant school. On the street I spoke English, at home German, and at school French. It was the most normal thing that from an early age, these three languages were like interchangeable hats dictated by the weather around us. I was blessed with a very happy childhood. My parents took my sister and me to a cottage in the countryside where we spent the summers on a huge lake in the Eastern Townships of Montreal, with endless hours of swimming, adventures in the forest, fishing, and good friends. Lake Memphremagog was like a character in a boyhood drama. I remember the dazzling sunsets that would fire up the glistening waters and the mist over the lake that was like a mirror in the early morning stillness. My mother had always encouraged us to be creative and we spent hours drawing, painting and making ceramic masks and objects that she would fire in her kiln. It seemed the most natural thing to dedicate my life to art.

Religion, on the other hand, had always been something rather vague; something that one was obliged to do, but which did more to limit one's creativity than anything else. I had very adolescent ideas about Christianity, and I had taken in a vague but decidedly retrograde picture of the Christian man. Perhaps this was due to the TV culture and some of the books I had read in High School. For instance, the obligatory reading in French class was Albert Camus, and Quebec writer André Langevin's sad novel, *Poussière sur la ville*. Both had pessimist passages about the loneliness of life on this earth. Existence was basically absurd, and the best thing to hope for in life was death, when there will be nothing but black non-existence. Although I did not really understand these books, they left a bad taste about religion. I remember being fascinated by an anti-war book by Dalton Trumbo called Johnny Got His Gun, about a First World War soldier who gets both his arms, both his legs, and his face blown off by a bomb. He is left like the stump of a tree, in total blackness, unable to hear, see, or speak. My memory of this book is that this stump of a man with absolutely no senses left to him, tried to communicate his desires to the outside world, but I don't recall him communicating with God. He did not pray. Or rather, if he did, it was not so important as passing a message to the doctors around his hospital bed. He eventually managed to send Morse code signals to the nurses by thumping his head against the pillow. All he wants is to be useful to others, despite having virtually nothing.

I was not a particularly good student, largely due to my own indolence. My parents wanted me to improve, so they sacrificed a lot to send me to an expensive boarding school where at age 14 I learnt better discipline, an openness to other cultures, and a certain detachment from the comforts of living at home. I would only come home once a month, and I came in contact with a number of students who had very difficult family situations. Stanstead was not openly religious, but it did have a certain generalized Protestant influence. Every morning the entire student body would assemble in the school Hall: a student was selected to read a preselected passage from Scripture. After announcements and the singing of the school hymn, we would all pray the *Our Father*. We all knew the school hymn by heart, *I Would be True*, by Howard A. Walter (1883-1918). I still remember a verse from the hymnal we'd sing. It read:

> I would be friend of all, the foe, the friendless.
> I would be humble for I know my weakness.
> I would look up, and laugh, and love, and lift.

That seemed to me the hapless nature of the Christian: the guy who just makes friends with the friendless, and with naive simplicity could only laugh and play like a bumbling clown. It wasn't inspiring.

The school had a policy that all students were obliged to go to a religious service every Sunday. It didn't matter which service you went to, but you had to get up and attend something. School "prefects" would be placed in every church where they would observe who entered, marking down the names of exactly who ended up where. If you failed to attend, you got a detention.

Of course in winter time, for many teenagers, Sunday was the sacred day not for going to church, but for skiing on the local hills. A bus would leave from the parking lot every Sunday at 9:30 a.m., so we had our Sunday "obligation" done in time to be on that bus. The local Anglican church had the earliest and shortest service. It was always packed with students from Stanstead wearing their ski gear. I still remember the embarrassment of seeing the collection plate make its way through the church packed with students and arriving back to the pastor with only three or four nickels. And then he'd raise up the plate giving thanks to God for the generosity of his people! Hardly any students went to the Catholic service in town. It was too late and much too long, lasting over an hour.

This was the superficial nature of my experience with religion. But that changed when I enrolled in a fine arts programme at Champlain College in St. Lambert. For the first time I encountered committed Christians. These were students in the fine arts program. For the most part they were Baptists. They were serious about their faith. They read the Bible and seemed very sure about the truth of their belief. What was even more striking was that they did not think that this was something only they should believe. They insisted that I too should make a commitment to believe and that my life would be a poor hapless bore if I did not embrace Christ.

One of the students that I became particularly close to was a fellow named Alain. He was tall, clean cut, and always well dressed. He was the best draughtsman in the class and could draw with great ease. He had a facility in painting and drawing that the rest of us envied. I became good friends with Alain and he was fun to be with. But he would often upbraid me when I would use the word "God" or "Jesus" in conversation. If I said something like "Oh my God", he would immediately stop me and say that this was taking the Lord's name in vain. Even if I said "Jeese, look at that beautiful painting" he'd stop me too: God, Jesus, Jesse, Christ, even the expression "jeewiz" were out of bounds for him, as well as for the others. It made me realize how often I used the name of someone whom I didn't even know. I had to figure out who this Jesus guy was.

Sometimes, while discussing religion, these Baptists would interrupt me when I said something that was true, and call out: "Praise Jesus!" I remember thinking about this on my own, but having very little sense of bearing about how true all this stuff about Jesus was. I was basically adrift at sea, with no compass, no map or sextant to guide me except my own feeling of what was right or wrong. I had no knowledge of the Bible and felt that I did not have the tools to make a responsible decision in favour or against having God in my life. I wanted to resist the idea of making a decision on this. I thought it would be something I would decide in my ripe old age. Or, in any case, later, not now.

The fallacy of this way of thinking came home to me one day in a conversation with a fellow art student. I don't remember her name, but she was rather unique because she was born without legs. She was older than most of us but undertook all the same projects in sculpture and painting that the program required. She did not let her handicap stop her. I still have this vision of her unabashedly dragging herself on the dirty studio floor, sawing a piece of wood, or chipping away at some plaster sculpture. Sometimes we had to pick her up and plop her back into her wheelchair.

I thought to myself, this woman obviously has had some experience in overcoming hardship. Maybe she can help me. I asked her one day over coffee if she believed in God. She looked at me from her wheelchair rather dryly and simply said: "I don't know, I haven't decided yet." I sipped my coffee. "So when are you going to make a decision?" I asked. She shrugged her shoulders: "I dunno. I'll decide after I die: if I die and he's there, then I'll believe in him; if he's not there, then I won't."

The logic seemed perfect, but somehow I understood that there was a deep problem with this rationale: to decide whether God exists after you're dead is just too late, period. It seemed like such a cop-out. Rationally, I couldn't really wait much longer and I felt more and more urged to make a decision, one way or the other. But I was afraid and I let the question drift away.

I never consciously prayed. It has occurred to me that in those years perhaps the closest I came to prayer was when I sang those German carols about the Christ child coming down to see us. I remember singing in front of the Christmas tree, which my mother had prepared with a lot of love. My father insisted that we use real candles on the tree (though we kept a bucket nearby just in case). This literally

186

made the tree come alive, and we could stare at its beauty for a long time. My father had an iron-clad rule: nobody was allowed to touch the gifts until we had finished singing all the hymns. As we sang, the tree seemed to speak to us. Little did I know that for Christians, it calls to mind the "tree of life" (cf. Gn 2: 9), and is a figure of Christ, God's supreme gift to humanity.

I had heard about Catholicism but the word simply conjured up images of the Spanish Inquisition, the burning of heretics, and unsavoury characters I had read about at school. My first real exposure to Catholicism was with my friend Dwight.

Dwight was a guy I had first met at scout meetings when we were quite young. He was about a year older than me; we also coincided during summer holidays on Lake Memphremagog. I knew his brothers and we used to play street hockey and other sports together. We spent hours together listening to music, going for walks, and sometimes visiting night clubs downtown. This was when I discovered that Dwight went to Mass every day. I would accompany him, sit beside him, and observe. He was discreet and did not preach about what he was doing.

I was struck by his piety. After every Mass he would take me to the altar railing, kneel down and say a short prayer he called the visit to the Blessed Sacrament. I stayed with him, more out of politeness and friendship than anything. He would also pull out an old tattered little book that he kept in his back pocket. It was a series of spiritual maxims called The Way by Josemaria Escrivá. He loved that book. It was totally worn out. He would read a point from this book, reflect a few minutes and then say an Our Father, Hail Mary and a Glory be. This is how I learned these prayers. I pretended to pray to please him.

One day, we were walking along a road in St. Lambert on the way to church. We had been talking quite enthusiastically about rock music, art, and poetry. Suddenly he stopped, he looked at his watch and stared at me: "Listen, we have 25 minutes to go before we arrive at church. That's just enough time to say the Rosary. I need you to help me to say the Rosary, because otherwise I'll get distracted and I won't pray well. You must help me". I didn't have a clue what the Rosary was. When I heard that it had something to do with the Blessed Virgin Mary, I told Dwight some vague objections that I had heard from my Baptist friends. He stopped all discussion: "That's okay Eric, you don't have to pray. You're just here to help me, that's all. I'll say the first half of the Hail Mary, and you the second half. Now repeat after me: Holy Mary Mother of God, pray for us sinners, now and at the hour of our death". It made sense: I was not actually praying. I was just helping Dwight to pray. So as a service to him, I memorised the Hail Mary, the Our Father, and the Glory be. I even learned the Creed and all the mysteries of the Rosary, which he dutifully explained to me one by one.

Later, I remember recounting this to my Baptist friends, and one was shocked, with a gesture of tearing his garment: "You worshipped Mary?" How could you do such a thing? In my defence I simply told him not to worry, I was not praying, I was just accompanying my friend, out of charity. Surely there can't be anything wrong with that? He agreed, if I was "helping" a friend, then it was okay. As a result, my first prayers to God and to the Blessed Mary were "pretend prayers" but I am now convinced that God heard them anyway and from then on slowly began to introduce his grace into my hardened soul.

One day I asked Dwight about the scourging at the pillar and the crowning of thorns. Why would people do such a cruel thing to Jesus, if they only disagreed with what he said. He told me that everything that happened to Jesus was not just the fault of those bad people. He looked at me: "It was your fault and mine too". What do I have to do with that, I asked? That was 2,000 ago! I certainly wouldn't have done that had I been there. Somehow he transmitted to me that we all hurt Jesus with our sins, even if they are committed now. I did not understand. But Dwight had a knack for throwing the ball into your court. He said: The reason you don't understand is because you haven't read the Gospel. If you had read the Gospel you'd understand. At home we had a Gospel but I seem to recall that it was in German, and printed in old Gothic script. Forget it, I thought.

Dwight gave me a Good News Bible. It was the entire Bible, and I had no idea where to start. So as I leafed through it, I saw that it was illustrated with wonderful little line drawings that fascinated me. They were similar to drawings by Henri Matisse who I thought was the greatest. Little by little I became intrigued by these simple illustrations. Some illustrated the Old Testament, others from the New. When I came across an interesting drawing, I would read around and find the corresponding story. I seem to recall that one of the first stories I read on account of the drawing was the story of the woman with a spirit of infirmity, who for 18 years had been bent over and could not straighten herself (*Luke 13,10*). I was attracted to the simple lines that showed this woman crouched down looking at the ground but going behind Jesus. It seemed to merge with the other story of the woman with the issue of blood who sought to touch the hem of his garment (Matthew 9, 20). When I read the stories I realized that somehow I was like one of those women: crouched over, just looking for material explanations to everything, not really looking up, all the time feeling the energy drawn out of me.

I began to read more and more. Suddenly I'd come across the mysteries of the Rosary that I had already learned in my treks with Dwight. I was struck by these stories, which were now so familiar. There was something in me that said that this was a good cultural education. It was good that I was learning this, but I could not make the leap to actually believe this God-stuff to be true.

My father said I was going through a normal phase and with time I would see that religion has brought a lot of interesting cultural enrichment but most of its influence was bad. He did not really explain this any further. I just know that his own father had converted to Catholicism sometime in the early thirties, and that he and his siblings had been baptized into the Catholic Church, but he did not remember receiving any instruction. His father was a medical doctor working in a field hospital near Breslau but disappeared at the end of the Second World War and was presumed dead. This left my father with a vague but decidedly bitter impression about Catholicism, perhaps because he felt that his own father had abandoned him. His mother saddled all the children over to the Lutheran church but without any instruction or practice of any kind.

I know that many people have received their vocation, special graces or been converted while traveling: St. Paul was converted on the road to Damascus; Mother Theresa saw her vocation while riding on a train and others. A decisive moment in my pathway towards God came on a country road on an ice-cold December morning near Lake Memphremagog. It was Christmas time 1981. I was 18. Dwight came by the cottage and we hitchhiked to Magog Mass 20 kilometres away.

It was a particularly cold and quiet Sunday. Most people stayed inside. Very few cars passed and nobody picked us up. After about an hour, my feet were freezing and we were far from home. Exasperated and tired, I told Dwight that we should think about turning around, going home and getting some hot chocolate. God would "understand" if we didn't make it to Mass today. Dwight turned to me and narrowed his eyes: "Why go back now? Haven't you been praying to the guardian angel?"

"The guardian angel?" I asked in disbelief. "Come on! That's just a medieval invention imposed on a credulous and ignorant populace", I said arrogantly. He raised his arms and said: "Ok, fine. Lets just wait five more minutes, and if the guardian angel does not come and help us out, then we'll go back as you say." I rolled my eyes and reluctantly agreed. Within 30 seconds of his proposal a large SUV suddenly appeared down the road and came to a stop in front of us, without us even making signs to it. Dwight turned to me with a slight smirk on his face, motioning to the car, he said: "After you, Mr. incredulous". I was still stunned when I entered the car. I felt the warmth inside and the comfortable seats and tried to focus on what just happened. It seemed like a direct intervention of the guardian angel, sent by God Himself to help us.

The man driving the SUV was dressed in ski apparel; in the front seat sat a young boy, about eight years old. We thanked him profusely for picking us up. He could see we were shivering. He asked us where we were going, and Dwight simply said we were going to Magog. But he inquired more, and asked where in Magog we wanted to be dropped off. For some reason Dwight wanted to stay discreet about going to church. But the fellow kept asking where in Magog, so Dwight relented and said we were going to Mass at St. Patrick's church. "Oh, I see, you're going to Mass..." and there was silence in the car. After some time the man said: "I haven't been to Mass in at least thirty years". Then he looked at his boy: "And I haven't even baptised you..."After another long period of silence the man exclaimed, hitting the steering wheel: "That's it, I've decided, I'm going to go to Mass again. It really has been terribly long. Do you think I could do that?" he asked Dwight. Dwight told him it wouldn't be a problem, and that maybe there would be a priest in the confessional. As we drove on through the winter landscape, Dwight muttered to me under his breath: "Keep praying to the guardian angel..."

When we arrived at the church, the man thanked us for giving him this idea, and he immediately entered the church without a word. We never saw him again. He simply disappeared into the crowd. By now I was in quite a daze, tired, and still a bit cold. I wanted to get into that warm church. It was a neo-Gothic style, with elaborately carved pews and a beautiful retable. The church was packed, and people were standing, since the Mass had already begun. Dwight led the way down a narrow aisle, advancing into the church looking for a free seat. Finally he spotted two free places. Before he entered the pew, he stopped dead and did something I was totally unfamiliar with but which was normal for any Catholic: he knelt down and made a slow genuflection, bowing his head reverently toward the tabernacle ahead. I had never seen this before, yet I was struck by his piety and reverence. As he stopped with his head down, I could see he was thanking God for bringing us safely to the church, and suddenly felt well up within me a deep sense of gratitude. Without knowing how or why, I too thanked God for bringing me to the warmth of the church. Right then and there, I did my first rather clumsy genuflection, copying Dwight, but, as I recall, drawing attention by my oddness. We stayed there until the end of the Mass. Dwight normally didn't leave Mass immediately. He always stayed giving thanks for the Eucharist, often well after everyone else had left. I did not yet understand the Eucharist, but I willingly stayed to give thanks. I intuitively understood that there was someone present to give thanks to. It seemed the most normal thing at this point.

Inwardly I felt a definite change. I discovered that God was not an idea. It was almost scary to consider that one could have a relationship with him; that he would be an active agent in my world. The guardian angel incident opened me to the possibility of God's direct action in my world. I knew people believed in God, and prayed to him, but I never thought that God would ever effect a real change or become an active agent in their lives. He was just "up there" where the stars shine. Why would he come in here and actually do something? But now with the incident on the road to Magog, I understood that he could be an agent in my life, that he could indeed act, that that he even had a definite plan for me. All this stayed very personal for me. I'm not sure I actually discussed this with Dwight. I now had a new vision of life, and I believed God had acted in my life. For the first time I started to pray the Rosary on my own, I'd look at a crucifix Dwight gave me, and I felt that God was in my life. But it was still rather nebulous and at the level of feeling.

Shortly after coming out of Mass I asked Dwight how one could justify belief in the infallibility of the Pope if history had shown that many of them had not lived very exemplary lives. Indeed some of them were positively "bad". Dwight did not address my question directly. He simply said that in any corporation, or in any business you need a boss, otherwise there is no coherent structure and everything is chaos. Basically, he said: The Pope is the boss. He keeps us all on the right track, and Jesus has given him a special grace to do that. Better to follow the Pope who has grace, than to follow your own ideas which are not much of a guarantee of anything. That was the answer I needed. It meant that I need not re-invent the wheel. God had revealed himself through Jesus Christ and given a special task to the apostles and to Peter to ensure that the message and the grace was passed on. Why would they not do that? They were just following the plan. From that moment on I trusted the Pope, and I felt I was Catholic. I only knew of few snippets of history and of doctrine, but I trusted that this principle was pretty straight-forward. Others had figured things out before me. Why complicate my life any further? Somehow I believed that this inner act of acceptance was enough for me to be Catholic. This changed a few weeks later after an off-hand remark in drawing class.

I remember one day sitting around with other students around a drawing table having lunch. The topic of religion came up, and different opinions were being bandied about on the value of practicing one's religion. One student compared the Protestants to the Catholics, another mentioned something about Buddhism's sense of peace. As the conversation went on, one student wanted to know what religion each of us professed. So one at a time each person would say their religion: one guy said he was Buddhist, another said he was Greek Orthodox, one girl said she was Baptist, and finally it was my turn to enunciate my religion. With great confidence I said I was Catholic. The girl next to me, her name was Rachelle, turned to me in disbelief: "What do you mean you're Catholic? You're not Catholic. You just think you're Catholic, but you're not actually Catholic. You haven't even been received into the Church, so stop saying you're Catholic."

I was dumbstruck. I vehemently protested, insisting that I believed the Creed, in the Pope, I prayed the Rosary, and that I even go to Mass, so therefore in my heart I am Catholic. Rachelle looked at me rather bemused and in a serious tone she said:

"Look, she said seriously, just because you do these things doesn't mean a thing. You haven't committed to anything. Becoming a Catholic is not like being a fan of the Montreal Canadiens. A fan is just a fan who knows how to cheer, but he doesn't play or win the game. He just sits on the sidelines, but it is the players that score the goals and win the game."

Dwight said I should see the local Franciscan priest where we habitually attended Mass. I had been going there for a while, so he was used to seeing me. At this point events get rather blurry in my memory, but I don't recall actually following an RCIA class. The priest gave me a catechism which I only skimmed through a few times. He felt that since I had been coming to Mass so regularly, I must surely be ready. No further explanations were

196

given, at least, not that I recall. So without much fanfare on a random Sunday in April 1982 I was received into the Church. I remember standing in front of the small congregation with a candle in my hand, and reciting the Creed. After I had said "Amen," everyone applauded and the priest gave me a huge Jerusalem Bible, which is still in my mother's home today. That was it. I remember thinking it was no big deal, since it was simply a confirmation of what I already believed. My parents sat at the back. That was the first time they had ever come into a church with me.

Years later I returned to Montreal as a priest, and had the great joy of presiding over Dwight's marriage in 2003. We now keep up regular contact, and I often thank him for being the instrument that led me to God.

# Jonathan Robinson

**Educated in Montreal, Edinburgh, and Rome. Fr. Jonathan Robinson is the Founder and Superior of the Oratory of St. Philip Neri, in Toronto. After ordination, he served as Cardinal Leger's English Secretary for the last four and a half years of the Cardinal's time in Montreal. He then taught Philosophy at McGill University. His books include *Duty and Hypocrisy in Hegel's Philosophy of Mind, On the Lord's Appearing, Spiritual Combat Revisited, The Mass and Modernity.***

## My Conversion

I was born in 1929 and received into the Catholic Church in 1954 when I was twenty-five, that is, fifty-five years ago and many of the events leading to my conversion date from well before that period. Nonetheless, the main lines of my journey to the Church are still clear to me. Furthermore, in the intervening years since 1954 I have reflected on my drawing towards, and being drawn to, the Catholic Church, and have several pages of notes on my spiritual journey. With the aid of my diaries and the notes I will try to present a faithful account of where I started and how I ended as a member of Christ's Church.

The interest in conversion stories, it seems to me, is in the account of the journey and not in the retelling of the journey's end. The end is the same in all cases; it is the gift of faith, the acceptance of the claims of the Catholic Church and being reconciled to Christ's Mystical Body. But the starting points from which men and women have reached this common goal are infinitely varied. It is the way the familiar arguments for Catholicism and the Church suddenly take hold of an individual that grips the reader. It is these starting points as well as the way the apologetic arguments suddenly became real and persuasive to the convert that anchor the different accounts into the real world and distinguish them from fiction. The fact that the account, no matter how imperfect it may be, began and developed in space and time gives to the convert's story an impact that a purely imaginary tale would not possess. There was only one St. Augustine, and there was only one Cardinal Newman, but any convert's story if he has tried to tell the truth, will bear some faint echo of these giants of the spiritual life; it will bear some faint echo because it will be an account, no matter how imperfectly it may be done, of the mercy of God operating once again in human history through the lives of individuals.

This account, then, is an attempt to retrace my steps to the Catholic Church; it says nothing about my subsequent history or about why, once having being received, I have never contemplated leaving the Church.

## My Family

When my Sister was a little girl she was asked why we were Protestant; to this she replied that it was because we were proud of ourselves. This may be somewhat inexact theologically, but it was the answer of a child brought up in a home where the parents knew who they were, and were more than content with what they were. My father was a successful lawyer from the Eastern Townships and a member of the Provincial Legislature; and my mother was from a well-known Montreal family. More importantly, theirs was a happy marriage; my parents loved each other and were loyal to each other. This experience of a solid marriage was, on looking back, the most important thing they gave us.

Neither of my parents needed to be socially ambitious and in fact they were not; I suppose it was a case of knowing who they were, where they had come from, and being quite content with this situation. Some of this sense of belonging came, in my father's case from what he thought of as his Loyalist background, and deep identification of his background in the Eastern Townships. What I learned as a child may in fact be bad history, but it is this history that has marked me. The Crown, the Empire, the Anglican Church as well as the perfidy of the Liberal party in Canada were all part of the mindset in which I was formed. It was a mind-set that has totally vanished from the Canadian landscape, but it went very deep where and when it did exist.

My Father's family came to North America in the 17th century to the Massachusetts Bay Colony.

The American Revolution found them in Newfane in the southern part of Vermont. When it became clear the Vermont was going to throw in its lot with the winning side the Loyalist Robinsons crossed the border and settled in Frost Village in the Eastern Townships in Quebec. Winter came early the first year the Robinsons were in Lower Canada and found them without windows or doors in their new home. They persevered, however, having little choice in the matter, and soon established themselves in Waterloo where, according to a memorial in St. Luke's Church, my great-great grandparents, Hezekiah and Selucia Robinson (née Knowlton) founded the Church of England in that town.

One of Hezekiah's sons was Jonathan, my great grandfather. He had five children: the story is that one of his sons emigrated to California and became a millionaire, another went to Montreal and also did very well financially, a third, Henry, became a professional organist. Henry became a Roman Catholic, and I remember my Father saying that the family took it very badly, and at the end of his life Henry used to place the blessed palm from Holy Week over his Mother's picture as a symbol of a reconciliation that never took place. The daughter married into the MacKinnon family and she was the mother of Mr. Justice Gordon Mackinnon of the Superior Court of Montreal.

My grandfather, the fifth child, stayed in the Townships and married the daughter of A.B. Foster, a senator in the first Parliament of the new Dominion. The senator built the railways south of Montreal and into Vermont, as well as some of the

Canadian Pacific Railway north of the Lake Superior. He was instrumental in the fall of one of Conservative Prime Minister MacDonald's governments; later the senator's downfall was engineered by MacDonald, and great indeed was great-grandfather's fall. In 1962 when I was a priest I went back to the house he had built in Foster which had become a school run by the Holy Name Nuns and said Mass for all those who had lived in the house; both for my family and for the Sisters.

My grandparents settled down to life in Waterloo where my grandfather inherited his Father's business which included 'the Old Stone Store' and a good deal of real estate. He was connected politically with the people who ran the County. This grandfather died in his early fifties leaving ten children. My father was I think about ten years old at the time.

My father was born in 1894 and was educated at local schools and at Bishop's College School in Lennoxville. During the Great War of 1914-1918 he joined the army and then transferred to the Royal Flying Corps. He was a Lieutenant by the end of the war, and several years overseas. When the war ended he went to Bishop's University Lennoxville followed by McGill and the study of law. He seems to have financed his studies with summer jobs and borrowing money from the rich Montreal relations. He used to have to collect the money from his uncle's house on Crescent Street. All his life my father had a chip on his shoulder about this branch of the family. He was called to the Bar and practiced in Montreal, and was well into his thirties when he met my mother whom he married in 1928.

My mother was twelve years younger than my father and was a MacMaster. Her family was connected with the MacMaster who founded the Steel Company of Canada, and one of her grandfathers, John Leeming, was an Alderman of the City of Montreal who in 1860 headed up the `Soirées and Concert Committee' which entertained the Prince of Wales. One wonders what the pleasure loving prince made of it all. John Leeming later declined the nomination to run as mayor of the city. By 1867 he was a Justice of the Peace, lived in a mansion on the North East corner of Dorchester and Guy – opposite the Grey Nuns. My Mother's people were all English speaking Montrealers, and if not at the very top they were firmly rooted in the Montreal economic and social scene. My grandfather, Andrew Ross MacMaster, was a lawyer. He was educated in Montreal, and earned his B.A. from McGill. He studied economics and political science at Edinburgh for a year, renewing his Scottish and Manx connections. He returned home to study Law at McGill. He started to practice law and had his own law firm. In 1917 my grandfather was elected to the Federal Parliament for Brome County in the Eastern Townships running as a `Laurier Liberal', that is someone who did not support the coalition government of Sir Robert Borden. As a result he was extremely unpopular with the English speaking of Westmount where he lived. Later on he became Provincial Treasurer in one of the Liberal Governments of Mr. Taschereau, and the member for Compton, another county in the Eastern Townships.

In 1936, my father was elected to the Provincial Legislature as the member for Brome County which my grandfather had represented federally, and was re-elected in 1939, 1944 and 1948. In 1944 he became Minister of Mines. His opposite number from Ontario was Leslie Frost who went on to be Premier of Ontario. As the only English-speaking member of the Provincial Cabinet, he had a sort of watching brief for almost everything involving English speakers in Quebec until his sudden death in 1948 just before his 54th birthday. Both my grandfather and my father left impeccable reputations of personal honesty and generous public service; in later years I found this a heavy burden to live up to.

## My Early Life

I was born in 1929 in Montreal and my sister in 1931. Until 1939 we lived at 8 Springfield Avenue in a row house on a short quiet street parallel to Sherbrooke Street in Westmount. We also had a house on Brome Lake in the Townships. In my memory there seems to have been more snow in those days, and one of my earliest memories is hearing my father piling the wood furnace with logs in the middle of the night. We skied, skated on the lake if the wind had blown the snow off the ice, went for sleigh rides and generally it was a wonderful happy time. These and similar memories are what are still uppermost in my mind. It was a happy and secure childhood; and although it was during the Depression this never impinged on our consciousness. There was a maid in the house to wash the dishes, keep things clean and do the household laundry.

After my father was first elected to the Legislature in 1936 we sometimes had a few days' holiday in Quebec. In those days there was a toboggan slide from the Citadel down to Dufferin Terrace, and we were also taken on exciting trips across the St. Lawrence, through the ice floes, to Levis on the other side and then back. We stayed in the Chateau Frontenac, and later on I remember being taken to the Garrison Club to eat.

I went to Roslyn School in Westmount until I was ten, and was sent to Bishop's College School. I never felt terribly at home there, but survived and began to adjust well enough. In 1939 father built a fine stone house on Westmount Boulevard. We lived there for only eight years and in 1947 my father, who was increasingly unwell from over-work, sold our house and rented a penthouse in a new apartment building on Atwater Avenue.

In 1944 I finished the Prep School at Bishop's, and rather than sending me into the Upper School, and without consulting me, father brought me back home to Westmount High School. I skipped a grade because of my time at Bishop's and had three not very successful years there. I read a lot, but these were in many ways wasted years academically. They were difficult years as well. My father although very successful in his legal and political life, was not well physically and was increasingly difficult to live with. This compounded all the usual male adolescent tensions with the father. He was constantly critical of what I did – and more for what I did not do. My sister claims I have not exaggerated in this. It ended up that I hated being at home in the holidays, except for the time I spent in the country at Knowlton and could go off by myself.

In 1945, when I was 16 I went to Bishop's University. I was too young to have been sent away to university, and I would have been much better off in a good high school with strict academic standards. I did well enough and came first in the Arts Division of the graduating class with a degree in Honours Philosophy. In June of 1948 I graduated with a B.A. and at the same Convocation father was awarded a D.C.L. *honoris causa*. I didn't really know what I wanted to do, so I asked if I could study Philosophy at McGill before starting law. If there was one thing that was clear in my parent's mind it was that I was going to end up as a lawyer; but they were prepared to wait and in the fall of 1948 I enrolled in McGill for an M.A. in philosophy.

## From My Father's Death Until My Conversion

In October of 1948 my father put his head into my room as he left for an inspection tour in the North of Quebec, and said so-long. I never saw him alive again. On October 11th, Thanksgiving Day, I was at Knowlton with five friends when my aunt came down from my grandfather's house to tell me that my father had died that morning. He had started to haemorrhage up North, was put on a plane and was dead by the time he arrived in Montreal. My mother was phoned to go to the hospital to meet him, and she arrived just in time to meet the ambulance. They came to tell her he was dead; she asked for water to wash his face and then went back to the apartment to cope with flying colours and a stony face with what had to be coped with.

Only someone who as an adolescent has lost a father or a mother through a sudden death can really understand the sort of devastating blow this was for me. It left me with an ineradicable sense of the fragility of human life and with an increasing scepticism as to the value of worldly success; or, perhaps more accurately, the value of sacrificing everything else to obtain what was so obviously evanescent. This may not have been an entirely healthy reaction from the psychological point of view, but it was certainly real enough; furthermore, it is a reaction I have never entirely shaken off.

After the funeral at Waterloo, in St. Luke's Church Waterloo, where my father had been baptized, we were driven home by our chauffeur and life changed dramatically. We found a new and smaller apartment on Sherbrooke St., and I had to pull myself together. In the spring I took three exams and did well. A year later I was awarded my M.A., the thesis was *The Coherence Theory of Truth in Bradley's Philosophy.* By this time mother's insistence that I study law had considerably weakened. Knowing that I would probably end up in politics her line now was that politics had killed her father and her husband, and she didn't want me going the same way unless I really wanted to. In fact, at one level she really did not care very much what I did, and felt overwhelmed by her own situation. Stoicism without religion had shown itself wanting as a way of life in her case.

A friend of my father's arranged for me to go to Ottawa to meet someone high up in the Department of External Affairs. I was very kindly treated, taken to the Rideau Club and back to dinner at the personage's house. Somehow, although I was fascinated by the prospect of the diplomatic life there was still the possibility of law and politics which interested me more. Furthermore, there were one or two questions still to be settled about the meaning of life so I decided to go on with philosophy.

R.D. MacLennan, the Head of the Philosophy Department at McGill, had been a pupil of Norman Kemp Smith's, the translator and commentator on Kant, and was for several years a major influence in my life. McLennan's own intellectual stance on life was a mixture of Scottish Calvinism and Kantianism. I admired him, but on the other hand, he had no answers for the sort of questions about the meaning of life and (especially) death which interested me. He thought I should go to Edinburgh for a Ph.D. With my M.A. under my belt, and the proper academic connections I could probably have gone to Oxford, but MacLennan had sent a favourite student of his there a couple of years before and the young man had fallen under Gilbert Ryle's influence, and more, generally the whole analytic approach, had done brilliantly, but then decided philosophy was all a waste of time. He didn't want a repeat performance on my part. So, in the fall of 1950, in my grandfather's footsteps, I went off to Edinburgh.

I sailed from Quebec on the Empress of Scotland, and had two years at Edinburgh, working hard at course work and my thesis. I pushed myself hard the second year and finished the thesis on *Bradley's Coherence Theory of Truth and its Relations to Kant and Hegel*. Then I went off for a month to Italy by myself, and fell in love with the country, but when I got back I found I would not be allowed to submit my thesis. I had tackled too much and tried to do it too quickly. My mother and sister had arranged to come over for my graduation, but came anyway. It was not a happy time.

I returned home that summer in the fall of 1952 and taught part time at McGill while I redid my thesis. I finally finished it in the summer of 1953 in the midst of a succession of deaths. I was hardly home when two of my uncles died. Then on New Year's Day of 1953, my father's oldest brother died and was buried from St. Luke's in Waterloo where we had all been baptized and from where we had buried my father. In the spring my sister was married in the same Church.

By the fall of 1953 my mother had firmly made up her mind that I was to do law. I didn't care too much and she controlled the purse strings. In fact, I enjoyed my first year of law and the winter of 1953-1954 was a sort of *annus mirabilils*. I was awarded my PhD, taught some philosophy and got through first year law at McGill coming 20th out of a class of 80. Later on I heard that the professors were very disappointed at my performance. The impression was mutual. With the exception of Frank Scott, I thought the intellectual calibre and integrity of the staff was not equal to the best of my philosophy teachers. Most of the law professors were academic and not practicing lawyers. That year I first learned to distrust academic lawyers with little or no experience of the practice of law, and my lack of enthusiasm in this regard has not changed much since. Still, all in all, it was a wonderful year. I decided that, after all, it was to be law and probably politics.

But then something happened which changed my mind. In about February (of 1954) the Head of McGill's Political Science Department asked me if I would be interested in working in the philosophy of law. Someone in the Rockefeller Foundation had seen that the philosophy of law was going to be an important subject in North America and the Foundation was looking for five or six students (as I remember it), trained in philosophy and law whom the Foundation would support for as long as was required to set the candidates up as Professors of Jurisprudence, or as independent thinkers. I was never entirely clear about exactly what the offer was all about, but there was the condition attached that I had to promise not to practice law.

I had no difficulty in saying no – my grandfather and father had been what I considered then, and still do, real lawyers; and my experience at the Faculty of Law had convinced me that I did not want to be an academic lawyer. Then very much to my surprise I was asked by the Rockefeller people whether I would like enough money to spend the summer at Oxford with no strings attached, although I ought to have some sort of a project. I had no trouble saying yes this time and said I would like to write an article on Lord Haldane's contribution to the work of the Judicial Committee of the Privy Council on the interpretation of the British North America Act; the British North America Act of 1867 being at that time (1954) the *de facto* Constitution of Canada. In addition to being Lord Chancellor, Haldane was an Hegelian philosopher of some note, and I saw my research as an opportunity to use my training in both philosophy and law to some effect. That was evidently enough for the head-hunters and I was given enough money to spend four months in England.

In May of 1954 I sailed for England and spent several wonderful months at Oxford. I lived at 17 Museum Road behind St. John's, had a pleasant room with windows on the front and was well taken care of by the land-lady. My friend Storrs McCall, from Montreal (who became a professor of philosophy at McGill) was at New College on a Rhodes Scholarship, and John Llewellyn (who is now a well-known authority on Derrida) a fellow-student from Edinburgh was at Trinity. I worked in the library of Merton College, where Bradley had been a Fellow, and at All Souls. Storrs and John brought me to several seminars and lectures – I had tea with Elizabeth Anscome who quizzed me about Solipsism and quickly terrified me into silence, tea again with Professor H. H. Price the authority on sense-data who talked about bird-watching, and I also went to some of Austin's seminars on words. At the same time I worked hard on the paper reading law reports and Haldane's works.

## Becoming a Catholic – Summer 1954

My father was an Anglican. He did, I believe, say his prayers and we were taught the Our Father and other prayers to say before going to bed at night. While we were growing up on Springfield we were taken to St. Matthias Church where I sang in the choir. Later on at Bishops College School there were daily prayers and Anglican chapel across the St. Francis River at the University chapel. The choir boys had red cassocks and white ruffs. Later at Bishop's University there was a daily celebration of the Eucharist as well as compulsory chapel five times a week – either Matins or Evensong, one could take one's choice. The English of the prayer book and the Authorized Version of the Bible became an intimate part of my consciousness, and the sober, structured Anglican liturgy of those days gave me a lasting distaste for the emotional and subjective in public worship. The beauty of holiness, and the Anglican liturgy of those days certainly possessed that, pointed beyond the personal and subjective to the transcendent God who was and is and is to come. It was a lesson, or a formation as the French would say, that has stayed with me since those days.

How deep did all this go? It was certainly more than a conventional routine as I always seem to have had a contemplative side to my nature. Aristotle said that philosophy began in wonder, and if the religious sense has the same source then I suppose I was deeply religious. On the other hand, this sense of awe and a desire to find out what was true and real was not enough to make a Christian (in anything but name) out of me for two reasons. In

212

the first place, I didn't believe in the Incarnation and in the second my stance on religion left me with a morality which was more Stoic than Christian.

The doctrine of the Incarnation teaches, to paraphrase parts of the Nicene Creed, that Jesus Christ was God of God, light of light, true God of true God … who for us men and for our salvation came down from heaven, took a human nature from his Mother the Virgin Mary, and became man. This is surely an astonishing series of propositions, and, once I grasped what was being affirmed, I found them not only astonishing but incredible. I suppose many people do when they really think about what the Creed says. My own particular difficulty always presented itself as a sort of existential terror at the magnitude of the universe in tandem with a deep sense of the absurdity of believing in a God (whatever, and whoever he might be) who would take any interest in the tiny spot of the universe we live in. Pascal's words that the emptiness of these vast expanses terrified him describes exactly my state; and this vertiginous sense of never-ending emptiness which always came accompanied by the overwhelming sense of the irrelevance of the earth and human lives made me want to run away and to drop the whole question of religion. I did my best to do just that; but I didn't quite bring it off.

So, as the question of the Incarnation seemed insoluble, and although obviously vital if I wanted to be a Christian, I adopted a practical policy of wait and see. The moral claims of Christianity seemed to be all that was left, and even here I was not persuaded that they were viable. I ended up with a morality whose imperatives were largely the conventional ones of truth telling, some sort of responsibility for those in need, and in my case, not surprisingly, given my background, a serious commitment to at least the ideal of honest public service. The failure to live up to these desirable qualities I viewed with various degrees of moral disapprobation. There was, however, no hint in my moral make up of a conscious sense of sin. Looking back, I now think that there was a sense of uneasiness or of something not quite right about my behaviour, but this would have been expressed in terms of what was inappropriate, not as an offence against God. I don't think in those years I was particularly bad, but I certainly had no real assent to the truth that Christianity was *the Way*; nor did I possess anything more than a vague sense that there was any direct and perhaps interesting connection between belief in Christ and what He demanded in every aspect of life both personal and social. Anglicanism, the Chapel, the prayer book and the Bible were aspects of life that were important, but then so was philosophy, music, my family and my father's career. Religion was an interest all right, but it was certainly not the only one. I do not think I ever seriously thought about becoming an Anglican clergyman.

My father's sudden death in October 1948 changed all that. I realized that my version of Anglicanism was of little use in dealing with a dead body. Anglicanism suddenly became all too obviously an adjunct to the political arrangements I had been brought up to believe in, arrangements that no longer seemed as important as they had. I remember buying a rosary and I began to go to the Catholic Cathedral in Montreal. Why that should have been the case is difficult to say. It had something to do with the fact that I detected a quiet note of assurance and authenticity that showed itself in worship that was clearly directed towards God; a God who was clearly taken to be a reality. There was, in those days at any rate, no hint that the real centre of interest was the edification of the faithful. Mass was about Immanuel, God with us; and this presence of the living God that was brought home to me time and time again, but never seemed to stay with me for very long. I recall thinking at Mass that this was where I belonged and I felt impelled to look for someone to instruct me in the Faith. But I had begun to know myself a bit better and was frightened of what I considered the emotional aspect of my pull towards Catholicism. Furthermore, actually believing in the Incarnation seemed as impossible as it ever had. Then, again, I had begun to appreciate the connection between Christianity and the way one was supposed to live. I had no intention of allowing my interest in religion to interfere with what I considered my own freedom to order my personal life as I saw fit.

I was in this half-way state from the time of my father's death until the summer of 1954. I also explored Anglo-Catholicism, but it was difficult for anyone with any sense of reality to think of the Anglican Church in Montreal as the true Catholic Church and to dismiss `The Romans' as a sect. Whatever the Catholic Church in Montreal was it was certainly not the `Italian Mission'. All that sort of argumentation might have made some sense in England, but it certainly made none in Montreal. The strong pull of Anglicanism, and it was very strong, was due to the fact that it was the only link that seemed to have remained from a happy and secure childhood. Of course, I realize that to be attracted to Catholicism and Anglicanism at the same time is logically contradictory; but ideas develop and attitudes change through a combination of thought and experience which includes all sorts of existential and logical absurdities. To `see things steadily and to see them whole' (as Matthew Arnold put it) is a achievement denied to most of us because it is something only the saints possess; the rest of us live on the basis of all sort of principles which on examination would be revealed as contradictory – that is just the way it is.

During my first stay in Edinburgh from 1950-1952 I read and talked my way out of Anglicanism. I had a fellow student, a Catholic whose mother was from the Rhineland, who pulverized what was left of my Anglicanism as a system. That was not, however, the same thing as convincing me of the truth of Catholicism. If there is a God, and if the Incarnation was somehow or other literally true, then, of course, Catholicism would follow. But was there a God? Did He become man? Did Jesus rise on the third day in as real a way as my father's dead body was really dead?

This was my condition when I went back to Montreal in the fall of 1952. I didn't have answers to my questions, and gradually the importance of trying to answer them became less overwhelming. The questions were still there, but as I couldn't answer them there seemed to be nothing left but to concentrate on law and politics. So it was that after my first year of law and the successful completion of my PhD, I had more or less decided to give up on any change in my religion. This was not because I didn't care so much as I thought that the caring was non-productive and was going to prove self-stultifying. I can't remember if I put it to myself in quite that way, but this was very much my state of mind when I went to Oxford in May of 1954. I wanted to be a success; I was going to be a success, although I still wasn't entirely sure what that meant for me.

Then I met the Dominicans at Oxford. They seemed to be everything I had been looking for. Blackfriars in those years was full of bright, learned men with a splendid liturgy who were prepared to talk to me and who understood my questions. They understood my questions and had the answers, or at least ways of dealing with the questions, but what they said just didn't click with me. I was grateful for their interest, very impressed with them as men, but it was clear to me, I kept telling myself, that what they stood for was not for me.

Then one morning in my room on Museum Road I had a searing experience of the presence of God and the reality of the faith that I could not deny and remain true to myself. I don't really know whether or not it was mystical in the strict sense of being a direct contact with God, but it was certainly paranormal. It didn't last very long, but while it went on everything, even the light itself, seemed vividly outlined. I didn't have a vision or really see anything except the extraordinary sense of vividness which was accompanied by a kind of pull towards a something. The experience cut very deep and left a profound and ineradicable impression. It was as though all the barriers which had prevented my becoming a Catholic were suddenly removed and I realized that I could now honestly ask to be a Catholic. This did not mean that the intellectual and moral difficulties had disappeared; it was rather that they had been put in their place because something new had been added.

I suppose what happened to me could be put technically in Thomistic language by saying that I had had an experience of God as the First Truth. In St. Thomas' account of the matter this First Truth is simple and undivided. The Christian revelation expresses aspects of this First Truth in propositional form, that is in language which the human mind can grasp and then go on to accept or reject. What I was given that day, the 'something new' that had been added was the gift of Faith in God the First Truth; that First Truth, which is expressed adequately and authoritatively but not exhaustively, in the Gospels and the teaching of the Church. From then on, in Newman's words, I understood that 'a thousand difficulties do not make one doubt'. I also realized I could go on as I had been, or make a radical change in my life. I said yes to the experience; and I acted on it by asking one of the Dominican students to find someone to instruct me. I believed then, and I still believe, that it was the grace of God which

218

moved me and I have never regretted my assent to this experience of the unseen, but almost palpable, presence of Christ.

I started instruction with Fr. Aelred Squire, O.P., and later with Fr. Leonard Boyle, O.P., and, although I enjoyed the time, nothing much about myself seemed to have changed. On September 15 I was received into the Church at St. Aloysius, Oxford, by Fr. Aelred. I spent the day before preparing for my first confession which I made to a Jesuit attached to the Church. Then, for a little while at least, I understood in an immediate way the words of Christ that He had come that we might have life and have it more abundantly. Nothing since that time has led me to doubt the fundamental rightness of having said yes to the grace of Christ. That of course is not the same thing as to say I have always found my way an easy one, or that I have been worthy of the gift.

# Jasbir Singh

**Jasbir Singh was born of Sikh immigrants to Canada. After studies in biology and in education, Jasbir moved to Japan in 1994 to teach. Returning to Ottawa in 1998, he went back to university to obtain a degree in software engineering. He has worked for the Royal Canadian Mounted Police as a technical writer and IT auditor, and at the Canada Revenue Agency as a quality assessor for software development and maintenance efforts. Jasbir was baptized and confirmed as a Catholic in 2003. Over a year later, he met his future wife, Lea, on Catholic-Match.com.**

## From Sikh to Catholic

At 5:36 a.m. on January 17, 1995, only five days before my 25th birthday, a major earthquake shook the city of Kobe, Japan. At that time, I was sound asleep in my bachelor apartment only a 20-minute commuter train ride away from the epicentre. Although news reports later stated that the 6.8 magnitude quake lasted for approximately 20 seconds, to me it felt like several minutes. It was long enough to change my entire life around.

When I awoke to the tremors and saw the light fixture swinging wildly over me like a pendulum, and heard the wooden beams of the building vibrating with a loud noise, I was sure that the building was about to crash down on top of me. I closed my eyes, curled up into the foetal position, and frantically repeated a Punjabi prayer that my mother had taught me when I was a child: "*Satnam Waheguru*"[29]. Death seemed only moments away.

Then just as suddenly as it had come, the shaking stopped, and I looked around me in disbelief. My apartment was in a shambles, with furniture overturned and dishes broken on the floor. As I surveyed the damage, I noticed that my portrait of Guru Gobind Singh, the last of the Sikh Gurus and a very important figure in the Sikh religion, had fallen from the table and shattered into a few pieces.

At the same time, only one small item in my apartment had remained peculiarly undisturbed. Some time ago, my friend Angelo had sent me a beautiful Christmas card: now, that card was the only one left standing, and Jesus gazed out at me peacefully from its cover.

Years later, this event came to hold much significance for me. I recognized it as an incredible miracle, an invitation from God to get to know him. As I was about to descend into the darkest period of my life, it was also a sign from Christ that he would be watching over me.

---

[29] Satnam translates to "God's name is truth", and Waheguru translates to "The Wonderful Teacher" in the Punjabi language. 'Wah' means 'wonder' and Guru is a term denoting 'teacher'.

But at the time, I didn't make much of the card incident: I was just happy to be alive. Over the next few weeks, as the aftershocks continued to rock the city, and as I discovered that 5000 people had died in the earthquake, I confronted my own fragile mortality. I kept thinking that I could die at any moment. I began to ponder the idea of living life to the fullest while I had my chance.

Why, I asked myself, had I been so timid all my life? Why was I blindly following the moral teachings that my parents had taught me, when I didn't even believe in their religion? Now I decided to be daring and bold, to try all the things I had avoided before – like the prodigal son, I was about to set out far from home.

## My Sikh Upbringing

In an actual sense though, I had already left my parents' home in Ottawa four months earlier, when I boarded an airplane headed for Japan. My parents had immigrated to Canada from Punjab, India in the late 60s. My father had come on a scholarship to complete his doctorate in economics at the University of Western Ontario in London (where I was born), and he soon launched on a successful career in the public service while my mother stayed at home to raise my brother, sister and myself.

My parents raised us to know our Sikh culture, as well as integrating into the Canadian culture. For instance, I didn't grow up wearing a turban. They also made the decision to cut my hair, although in the Sikh religion, one of the central practices is that men are never supposed to cut their hair. Nor did I wear the traditional dagger (the "kirpan") that fully practicing Sikhs wear under their garments, as a symbol of readiness for self-defence. I did however wear the Sikh bangle (the "kara") around my wrist, thus identifying myself as a Sikh.

We were a part of the Sikh community, and we went to the Sikh temple (the "Gurudwara") occasionally – perhaps a couple of times per month. While I liked to go and play with my friends at the Gurudwara, I didn't care for the religious and ceremonial aspect of it all. The hymns were all sung in a difficult poetic Punjabi language, which I did not understand, and I always had the sense that the congregation was blindly following customs and rituals that few people actually understood. When I asked my parents to explain them, I became even more frustrated when they told me that this is just how it was. They were not able to provide me with a satisfying response.

Later, when I was a teenager, I read more about the Sikh religion on my own, and for a while I was proud to be Sikh, mainly because of the history of Sikhism. The founder, Guru Nanak, had brought a revolutionary thought to a Hindu India steeped in sharp conflict with Islamic invaders. He preached that there was no Hindu or Muslim, that all men were brothers first. He rejected the rigid Hindu caste system, so that the Sikh religion recognized all people as equal.

However, the teachings of the Sikh religion still did not seem believable to me. I read some of the translated Guru Granth Sahib (the Sikh holy book), and I was not convinced that it was divine. Some of my basic questions just weren't answered, or if they were, I didn't take the answers seriously. For example, I just didn't believe that man would be reincarnated as other humans or as animals in another life if they were not "good."

I came to understand Sikhism mainly as a code of conduct rather than a religion. It was the moral values that we had, as well as the practices and rituals, that made us distinct. But in the end, that was not enough to keep me interested in practicing the Sikh religion. As I neared my 20s I stopped attending the Gurudwara except for special occasions once or twice a year. Sikhism became merely my cultural identity. I still obeyed the cultural moral teachings, mainly out of obedience to my parents, but otherwise my outlook on life was completely non-religious.

Far more attractive than the Sikh religion was the Western culture around me. Like most young men, I was interested in young women and in sports, and eventually, in developing a teaching career. After graduating from university and obtaining my high school teacher's license, I hopped on a plane to Japan, partly to gain teaching experience, and partly to escape the semi-arranged marriage that seemed inevitable if I stayed in Ottawa.

## The prodigal son in a foreign land
Four months after I landed in Osaka, the Great Hanshin Earthquake tumbled down the moral precepts that I still obeyed. From then on, living life to

224

the fullest meant turning away from the traditional values that seemed purposeless and too limiting. Psychologically, it was also the moment when I broke free from the power that my mother's moral rules had over me. She would no longer be my conscience, and I would no longer measure my actions mainly by a desire to avoid disappointing my parents; I would now make my own rules, and become a man. Ironically, I rationalized my way into the darkness by thinking that now, I would answer only to God – a god whom I did not know.

The first decision I made was to kiss a woman for the first time. The Sikh culture does not approve of dating, and having a girlfriend was forbidden, so until that time I had never been romantically involved with a woman. These prohibitions had upset me, but I had followed them all throughout high school and university, even as I struggled with the sense that there was something wrong with me for not experiencing these things like my secular friends did. But after the earthquake, I became fixated on the thought that I could not bear to die without ever having kissed a woman. I was no longer willing to wait until marriage for that to happen.

Of course, kissing a woman became just a step to much more. Like the prodigal son, I began a life of immoral and "loose living." My life was based on the "pleasure principle" of enjoying myself as much as I could. I saw women as objects to fulfill my self-gratifying search for happiness. I even convinced myself that I was a moral and progressive person while doing these things. And yet, happiness escaped me. The pursuit of physical pleasure left me with no lasting joy. Instead I constantly found myself unsatisfied and frustrated. My behaviour was hurting me and rotting me out from the inside. I spiralled down towards spiritual death.

After four years of this life in Japan, I decided to return to Ottawa – not because of any change of heart, but because I missed my family, and I was starting to think about settling down and having a family, which I only wanted to do in Canada.

## The Search for a True Faith

Moving back in with my parents, and being surrounded once again by friends and family, caused me to take a deeper look in the mirror and to reflect on the life I was leading. I sensed that I was on the wrong path, I recognized the suffering of my empty existence, and I began to long for a greater meaning in life. In fact, I began to call out to God for the first time, wanting to know him without realizing it. Briefly I revisited Sikhism, but once again it did not hold the answers to my questions (Who is God? Why did he create the world? Why did he create us? What was the purpose of life? Etc.), and I started to explore the teachings of other religions.

The Eastern philosophies were appealing to me at the time, but they also fell short of convincing me. It was clear to me that their writings were simply man-made, and not good enough to be divine. At that time, I did believe in some kind of God, but I concluded that he was simply too far out of reach and unknowable by man. Every wise man's explanation was just an attempt at building a ladder (some perhaps taller than others), but there simply was no ladder tall enough to reach God.

When I failed to be convinced by the Eastern religions, part of me resigned to the belief that there was not much more to life. I didn't even think about studying Judaism, Islam or Christianity – in fact, although I considered myself to be open-minded and tolerant, Christianity had always been repulsive to me in some ways. I thought that Christians were arrogant because they believed that all non-Christians would go to hell. It also seemed ridiculous that they believed God could become something as limited as a human being. More than that, over time I had also acquired a subtle hostility towards Christians. I considered them closed-minded and resented their efforts to proselytize.

## A Glimmer of Hope

Nearly four years after moving back to Ottawa, on a coop work term assignment while completing my engineering studies at the University of Ottawa, I became interested in a young coop student named Stephanie. We had dinner together a couple of times and soon, our conversations began to revolve around religion. It turned out that she was a devoutly practicing Catholic, and strangely, I was not turned off by that revelation as I had been in the past. Instead, I was oddly drawn to what she had to say, and soon found myself seriously contemplating her words.

Over many lunches, we discussed religion and God. At first I thought that I was going to teach Stephanie something about religion, but it quickly became evident that she was deeply challenging my own ways of thinking while I was making no progress in disturbing her inner peace.

For instance, I remember asking her how she could believe that God would only allow those who believed in Jesus Christ to gain entry into Heaven. Stephanie explained that those who hadn't heard of Jesus through no fault of their own would not be judged by God according to the same standards as Christians, who would be held more accountable for their sin because they had the privilege of knowing the full truth. This was interesting to me because it dispelled my previous understanding that Christians believed all non-Christians were destined for hell.

On the other hand, when I tried to convince her that all religions had their own equally valid path to God, and that most people could get into heaven as long as they were "good", Stephanie insisted that the door to heaven was narrow, and only a few entered (later I realized this was based on Matthew 7:13-14). Could it be that she was right?

Another objection I had to Christianity was that it seemed simply impossible that Jesus, a living man, could be God in the flesh. He may have been a good preacher, but God? But now I started to realize that this unbelievable teaching was actually what made Christianity fundamentally different from all the other religions that I had rejected as man-made. While those other religions had wise men like the Dalai Lama, Guru Nanak or Mohammed, who tried to build ladders up to God, Christianity was the reverse: it taught that God himself chose to come down to our level in the form of a man to bridge the gap. This gave the Bible much more authority than could be found in the other religions. If a person truly believed that Jesus Christ was God, then his teachings (God's own revelation to us) would be far better than anything a man could invent on his own. They would be the ultimate truth. Other religions seemed easier to believe because the founders did not claim to be God, but I was not interested in those religions precisely because they seemed man-made. Christianity made the most radical claim I had ever encountered, and it was the hardest and most difficult religion to believe because of this very point. However, I realized that if one did believe that Jesus Christ was God, then the teachings of Christianity would be far more convincing than other religions. Moreover, wasn't anything possible for God? If He truly was omnipotent, I had to admit that he could decide to become a man if he really wanted to, no matter how ridiculous and unbelievable.

We also discussed many other questions that I had about Christianity. Stephanie's explanations were new to me, and they planted seeds in my mind. Why did this practicing Catholic woman seem to have all the answers? I sensed that God was somehow closer to her than to me, and I knew it had to do with her being a Christian.

## God's Touch

Looking back, it is clear to me that God prepared me for this encounter for at least eight years. My dissolute life had brought me only unhappiness and inner emptiness, and had provoked an unsuccessful search for God in other religions. Even as I continued to walk in utter darkness, I had recently started attempts to reform my life. I was parched for meaning and for truth, and a glimmer of hope remained that I would somehow find both of these. Although I didn't yet know it, my heart was longing for Jesus, and it was ready to find him. Now when I met this Christian woman, her words touched me far more deeply than I had ever expected.

It did not take long for me to open myself to Jesus completely. After so many years of doubt and darkness, I started to question my resistance to Christianity. One winter evening in 2002, only a few weeks after meeting Stephanie, as I was returning home on the evening bus, I went through an intense internal struggle. I was deeply attracted to the certainty and peace that this Christian woman seemed to have from her religion, and I wanted to experience it for myself, but the only way was to open myself to discovering Christianity "from the inside" the way she understood it. I had been willing to do this in Japan with the Japanese – I had tried new things and experienced their world without reserve. Why not do the same thing with Christianity?

I wondered what would happen if I let down my guard and stopped resisting Christianity. What if I let Jesus in? I challenged myself in the silence of my own mind, and built up the courage to try a thought experiment. Without expecting anything, I decided to say: "I love Jesus".

What was originally supposed to have been a simple thought experiment turned into something spectacular. As soon as I pronounced the words, a flood of energy entered into me. I felt a warm sensation in the core of my body, my chest was burning, the hairs on the back of my neck stood on end, and right there on the bus, I started to weep with overwhelming joy. Was it God? Did he actually touch me? It was as if my soul had awakened for the first time, and I had experienced something beyond this world.

That evening, for the first time, I opened up the New Testament and began to read with a completely open mind, not as a sceptic. The events described in the Gospels were immediately real to me, as if I were actually present in the background, witnessing everything that Jesus had said and done. The parables overwhelmed me with their wisdom, and the miracles and healings performed by Jesus left me awestruck: only God could do such things.

Late in the night, I came across the passage where the disciple Thomas faces Jesus after the resurrection. At that moment, Jesus was speaking not to Thomas, but to me: "Put your finger here, and see my hands; and put out your hand, and place it in my side; do not be faithless, but believing." (John 20:27)

I found myself falling to my knees together with Thomas, and I also answered: "My Lord and my God!" (John 20:28) Suddenly I believed: I knew that I was reading the Word of God to his people. I had found the truth. It was like a light switch had turned on in my soul. I had been blind, but now I could see. I felt myself falling in love with Jesus Christ, the Way, the Truth and the Life!

That night, I knew that I would become a Christian.

## Discovering a New World

Now began an intense period of my life when I learned a great deal about Christianity and Catholicism, soaking up all I learned like a sponge. I used the Internet to research the history of the Catholic Church, the Catholic understanding of heaven and hell, views on abortion, contraception, the death penalty, and many other points of information. I also explored Protestant faiths, but quickly decided that this incredible multitude of branches had strayed from the root of the tree. I wanted to learn straight from the original source, and that could only be the Catholic Church, built on an unbroken line of apostolic succession ever since Jesus had appointed Peter as the head of the Church.

One Sunday, I accepted Stephanie's invitation to attend mass at the Notre Dame Cathedral in Ottawa. I was impressed at how simple and easy it was to follow, compared to the services at the Gurudwara. And yet, there were also interesting similarities between these two services. After the mass, I saw an African priest in the pews and we nodded at each other. I felt drawn to speak to him, and nervously approached him to introduce myself. He was friendly, and we exchanged a few words. It was just a simple meeting, but for me it was extremely significant. After exiting the Cathedral, I sat on a bench and wept for some minutes, overcome with the recognition that I had taken the major step of attending mass and had even made contact with a priest.

Stephanie had grown up in a Catholic faith community that was centered around a monastery in Shawinigan, Quebec. Approximately 10 religious brothers and 10 religious sisters lived there and practiced a very disciplined routine that included a daily Liturgy of the Hours and rosary. The families of the community regularly attended retreats at this monastery, and eventually I was invited to join one of these retreats. There, I listened to the head brother, Frère Pierre, give interesting talks about Catholic history and how to be a good Catholic.

I greatly enjoyed the talks, but even more touching were the people and families who congregated at this monastery. I met several large Catholic families who seemed very happy and beautiful. Their children were so loving, obedient, and affectionate, so intelligent and well behaved. They never complained and genuinely participated in the retreats. They sang, played musical instruments, and performed skits in front of their parents. I had never seen such examples of well functioning and prayerful families, and I knew that these were the fruits of their devoutly lived lives of faith.

Through these families, I also gained great admiration for the Catholic perspective on death. In Sikhism, death is considered a serious tragedy, even though it is believed that the person will reincarnate as another person or animal. Growing up I had seen mourners wailing at funerals in unbounded displays of sorrow. This was partly why death was a subject I liked to avoid, as I never knew how to deal with it.

But these Catholic families handled death very differently. When a young child in the community died unexpectedly, I decided to attend the funeral despite my usual reservations. When I arrived, I learned that the service was not being called a funeral but rather a "ceremony of angels", because in the Catholic religion, an innocent, baptized child is believed to go directly to heaven when they die. This was a completely new concept for me: a ceremony to celebrate one's entry into heaven! Witnessing this positive way of dealing with death further demonstrated to me the fruits of Christianity.

## Becoming a New Man

Like these families, I began to pray the rosary daily, visit the monastery on a fairly regular basis, and the head brother became my spiritual advisor. It was then that my toughest and most difficult internal battles with vices and sin were fought.

Having read the Gospels and learned about some key Catholic teachings, I had become aware that I had been living an immoral life. I now knew that "every one who looks at a woman lustfully has already committed adultery with her in his heart" (*Matthew 5:28*), and St. Paul's words had touched me when he said that God's will was:

> that you abstain from fornication; that each one of you know how to control your own body in holiness and honour, not with lustful passion, like the Gentiles who do not know God...
> – *1 Thessalonians 4:3-5*

and when he said:

> But I say, walk by the Spirit, and do not gratify
> the desires of the flesh. For the desires of the flesh
> are against the Spirit, and the desires of the Spirit are
> against the flesh; for these are opposed to each other,
> to prevent you from doing what you would.
> – *Galatians 5:16-17*

Like Adam and Eve, who realized that they were naked and hid from God after eating of the forbidden tree of knowledge, I now felt ashamed for having offended God with my past sins. Together with the Prodigal Son, I crumpled myself at my Father's feet and cried out "Father, I have sinned against heaven and before you; I am no longer worthy to be called your son." (Luke 15:21)

In response, the Father gave me a new chance to live a virtuous life. Yes, I wanted to change my ways. But overcoming my tendencies was not always an easy process. I had previously been a slave to sin, and it took me several months of great struggle to resist the temptations to fall. It was only God's sanctifying grace through the intercession of the Blessed Virgin Mary that helped me to successfully defeat the vices that had a grip on my soul.

Once I had finally won, I felt incredibly free! I was no longer a slave. I was completely healed! I started to see the world with new eyes. Rather than viewing women as objects of pleasure and lust, I had a new understanding of the true and proper relationship between man and woman, and I had a new respect for women as human persons. But most of all, I had a newfound understanding of myself and the dignity of the human being. This understanding was also further developed by my growing love for Christ and devotion to the Blessed Virgin Mary.

## Baptism

In the fall of 2002, I enrolled in the RCIA program at St. Patrick's Basilica in Ottawa. For me, those classes were far more than a formality. Fr. Lindsay Harrison, who led the reflections and discussions, provided an excellent and in-depth overview of Catholic teachings and brought together everything that I had read in the New Testament and learned at the monastery in Shawinigan.

On April 19, 2003, I was received into the Catholic Church at a beautiful and profound Easter Vigil mass that will stay forever vivid in my memory. My baptismal name: Thomas.

## The Sword of Division

Jesus told us:

> Do not think that I have come to bring peace on earth; I have not come to bring peace, but a sword. For I have come to set a man against his father, and a daughter against her mother...and a man's foes will be those of his own household. He who loves father or mother more than me is not worthy of me.
> – *Matthew 10:34-38*

Those words came to have literal meaning for me. Soon after I started attending mass, before ever getting baptized or becoming a Catholic, my family had a strong negative reaction to my new interest in Christianity. Their perspective was understandable, in that the Sikh religion was founded to oppose the religious conversion that Muslims had forced upon Hindus. My family held the view that religious conversion was wrong, and that people should stay in whatever religion they are born into. Moreover, Christianity was held in particularly negative esteem by my parents, partly due to its missionary and colonialist history in India. So my interest in Christianity was seen as a betrayal of my family, faith and culture. What's more, it was simply incomprehensible to my family that I could actually have come to believe the seemingly absurd claims of Christianity – they believed that I had been brainwashed.

But even as I had to move out of my parents' home, and as I faced many tearful and tense confrontations with my parents, I was ready to carry any cross that Christ wanted me to carry. I completely trusted him and was determined to follow him anywhere. In my mind, I knelt down on one knee before him like a subject before his king, completely devoted and ready to lay down my life for him.

Things were very tense in my family for many months during the time when I completed my conversion and began my new life as a Catholic. However, over time, my parents have come to be more accepting of my choice to follow a new path. I never stopped loving them with all my heart, and I continued to show them the good fruits that my conversion was bringing into my life.

One of these fruits, I believe, was my marriage. Early in 2004 I began to pray a special devotional prayer to St. Raphael for the intention of finding a faithful Catholic spouse. At the end of that year, God decided to present me with a beautiful Czech-Canadian woman named Lea on a website called CatholicMatch.com. We were married at St. Patrick's Basilica on July 1, 2006, and are now expecting our first child.

Since my marriage, the tension in my family has lessened dramatically as many happy events and family joys have overtaken the tears of the past, and the relationships in my family are healing.

## A Conversion that Lasts a Lifetime

To this day, it continues to amaze me how I was transformed. God never gave up on me during the course of my life, even as I put too much stock into my own beliefs and relied heavily on my own logical reasoning and standards. I didn't know how far off I was from God and the moral laws that He established for us. But His love and mercy knows no bounds, and He offers it to us freely. I blindly called out to Him in the darkness, and He brought me out of the pit of destruction and set my feet upon rock (Ps 40).

Discovering the faith is a process that lasts a lifetime. There are so many incredible resources available to us that help to deepen our faith and to increase our knowledge and understanding of Catholic teaching. In the last couple of years, my wife and I have found spiritual enrichment and guidance through the Opus Dei community in

Ottawa. We also enjoy reading spiritual works together and praying in the little chapel that we have
set up in our home. We look forward to sharing our
love for Christ with our children.

## Abandonment to God

> Ask, and it will be given to you; seek, and you
> will find; knock, and it will be opened to you. For
> every one who asks receives, and he who seeks finds,
> and to him who knocks it will be opened.
> – *Matthew 7:7-8*

My greatest wish is for the non-Christian reader
to know that the hope Jesus Christ offers each one
of us is far beyond anything that this world has to
offer. I truly believe that He is God the incarnate,
and He visited us once to offer us salvation and
hope for eternal life. Anyone who makes a sincere
effort to open up their mind and heart to Jesus
Christ will find their way. All that one has to do is
to abandon oneself and take a leap of faith. The
following prayer by Charles de Foucauld has helped
me to do just that throughout my conversion journey:

> *Father,*
> *I abandon myself into your hands;*
> *do with me what you will.*
> *Whatever you may do, I thank you:*
> *I am ready for all, I accept all.*
> *Let only your will be done in me,*
> *and in all your creatures.*
> *I wish no more than this, O Lord.*

239

*Into your hands I commend my soul;*
*I offer it to you*
*with all the love of my heart,*
*for I love you, Lord,*
*and so need to give myself,*
*to surrender myself into your hands,*
*without reserve,*
*and with boundless confidence,*
*for you are my Father.*
*Amen.*

# Lars Troide

The author is a semi-retired Professor of English Literature at McGill University in Montreal. A native of Connecticut, he received his B.A. and Ph.D. from Yale University. His professional achievements include two U.S. National Endowment for the Humanities Research Fellowships (1980 and 1998) and 25 years of funding from the Social Sciences and Humanities Research Council of Canada.

## My Winding Road to Rome

You could say that my spiritual odyssey began in Sweden. My parents, Eleon and Dagmar (Wahlberg) Troide, were born there, my father in Stockholm, my mother near Hammardal far to the north. Inevitably, they were raised as Lutherans. They actually met in Connecticut after emigrating separately to the States. They married in Stamford, Connecticut, in 1930, and I was born there, their second son, on June 15, 1942.

Three months later, on 25 Sept., I was baptized by Pastor Norel Gustafson in St. John's Lutheran Church. My mother's sister Ina and her husband, Rowland Hill, stood as witnesses. Of course, I don't remember that event, but I still have the Memento and Certificate of Baptism, filled out in a beautiful script by the pastor and passed down to me by my mother.

My first conscious memory of religion is a Sunday service when I was maybe four. The new minister, Pastor Johnson, had worked himself up to a suitable pitch of fervour in his sermon and emphatically pronounced the name of "Jesus Christ!" I immediately piped up in my childish voice, "Mommy, he said a swear word!" The congregation laughed, the minister dutifully smiled, and continued his sermon.

As I write these words, I am led to think that they reflect an important fact of my early upbringing. The extent of our prayer life at home was a rhymed Swedish prayer for children which my mother taught me to say by rote. I can still recite the prayer (in Swedish) from memory, but having never really learned to speak or write Swedish, all I can give here is a prose paraphrase in English of the beginning and end: "God, who keeps the dear children: help me, who am little... The storm lies in God's hands." As a child, I never knew what the prayer meant! But my mother did give me a strong moral education (my father was largely silent), enjoining my little soul never to lie, cheat, or swear (as witness my outburst in church).

My next "religious" memory was the literally sunlit day when my mother asked me if I would like to attend Sunday School (notice she didn't tell me to do it). I was five. I eagerly agreed, and for the next eight years was a regular Sunday

School student. And at 13 I was confirmed in the Lutheran faith.

*

Pastor Johnson, still our minister, who presided at the confirmation, actually asked me if I felt any calling to the ministry. I was a good student in school and clearly had the necessary intellectual gifts. But the seed of faith planted at my baptism still lay dormant. Through my high school years I slowly drifted away from the church, and eventually stopped attending Sunday service. My parents, both because of ill health and increasing spiritual luke-warmness, also stopped going.

In college (Yale, to which I had won a scholar-ship), my only "flirtation" with God was when I served as a reader at the French language evening services in the university chapel. I was encouraged to do this by my French instructor, Jacques Bos-sière, who had been a Catholic priest but had turned Episcopalian and married a French Canadian lady. In fact, I had studied a great deal of science in high school and college (physics, chemistry, biology, and geology), and was increasingly influenced by a skeptical scientific world-view. As a result, by the time I graduated from Yale College (in 1964), I was pretty much a confirmed "agnostic." As I learned later, "agnostic" is a term coined by Charles Dar-win's so-called "bulldog," Thomas Henry Huxley, but is in fact practical atheism, as was pointed out by C.S. Lewis and others.

As I look back on my life, I see that my em-bracing of agnosticism was the result of my placing too much confidence in science as a mode of

243

knowing, and also a result of overweening pride and self-centeredness. If we do not believe in God, we tend to believe too much in ourselves. Life-long friends tell me that I always seemed to them a "nice guy," but inside I was certainly an intellectual snob and a seeker after immediate self-gratification. In my case gratification came largely from seemingly innocuous things, like books and classical music. But the fact remains that I thought too highly of myself, and not enough of the needs of other people, whether family, friends, or the people in my community or around the world.

I did have a good degree of patriotism. My mother, who was born and raised in a poor farming community in Sweden, was especially grateful for the opportunities she had received when she came to America (she eventually became a licensed practical nurse). I cut my teeth on the concept of "the American Dream." So when I went to college, it was with a whole-hearted belief in the obligation of every citizen to serve his/her country in some tangible way. My way was to enrol in the Army ROTC program at Yale (since regrettably dropped because of the short-sightedness of anti-war elements at the university). The day I received my B.A. (in English literature), on 22 June 1964, I was also commissioned a second lieutenant in Army Intelligence.

I was allowed to defer my active service since I had been accepted into the M.A. program at Columbia University in New York City. But after a year at Columbia I decided to go on active duty for the required two years. In Feb. 1966 I finally went to Fort Benning, Georgia, to receive training as a platoon leader, prior to my going to Fort Holabird, Maryland, for my intelligence training.

\*

By what may have been an act of providence, after five weeks at Fort Benning I was afflicted with a generalized rash over my whole body. The Army diagnosed my condition as "chronic nummular eczema," reclassified me as 4-F, and sent me packing back to civilian life. I say "act of providence" because the U.S. was just entering the hotter stages of the Vietnam War, and I almost certainly would have ended up there. According to the Army's needs, I could have been a platoon leader instead of an intelligence gatherer, and the average life expectancy of a platoon leader in Vietnam was two weeks! And though my condition was allegedly "chronic," I had never had it before, and I have never had it since.

I know now that God has a purpose in life for each and every one of us. Whatever that purpose is, however grand or humble it may be, we sanctify it by pursuing it with total dedication. My senior year at Yale my parents, who had been helping me financially but were not well-to-do, asked me to take on a part-time job at the university. I applied late, and there were only two jobs still available. Since I was an English major, I chose to go to work, nine hours a week, for the Yale Edition of Horace Walpole's Correspondence. Walpole was an important 18th-century British literary figure. I did not know, when I first entered the office of the Walpole Project in the Yale Library, that this would turn out to be the opening chapter in my life's work.

I was greeted by the Project's kindly associate editor, Dr. Warren H. Smith, who would become my life-long friend. I would soon meet the Project's founder and editor-in-chief, Wilmarth Lewis, a wealthy man who had dedicated his fortune and his life to promoting the modern reputation of Walpole (1717-97), who was a politician, connoisseur of the arts, author of the first Gothic novel, The Castle of Otranto, and writer of voluminous familiar letters that give a sweeping panorama of life in 18th-century England. Lewis had begun the Yale edition of Walpole's correspondence in 1930. A massive undertaking with 12 different volume editors, it would eventually be published in 48 volumes between 1937 and 1983.

My initial job was as a humble typist of the volume editors' annotations. Soon enough I was trusted to run into the Yale library stacks to track down and double-check for accuracy the sources of every annotation in the current instalment of volumes being worked upon. This training taught me a deep respect for the absolute integrity and factual accuracy that characterize true scholarly work. The job of the editor of familiar letters is to provide the necessary context, whether it be identifying an acquaintance Walpole met, finding the source of a literary line quoted by him, explaining a political event touched on by him, or whatever. The value of such work depends on a scrupulous and honest attention to detail, without which the annotations dissolve into a kind of hazy impressionistic mist.

After my senior year at Yale I stayed in friendly contact with Dr. Smith, but left the 18th century for the field of 20$^{th}$ century literature at Columbia. However, after leaving the army, completing my M.A. at Columbia in 1967, and a year teaching at a boys' preparatory school in upstate Connecticut, I visited Dr. Smith in the Walpole Office at Yale, to be told that a volume editor had unexpectedly resigned, and would I be interested in taking over his work? My Columbia M.A. and my prior Walpole work were considered promising credentials. As a result, on 2 Sept. 1968 I began full-time work as editor of Walpole's correspondence with his cousin Henry Seymour Conway (an army general and secretary of state), volumes 37-39 of the complete edition.

Within a few weeks I discovered that I was born to do this kind of work. I am gifted with a capacious memory for detail and an insatiable curiosity about the large and small particulars of everyday life in earlier societies. I quickly became a specialist in English history, 1763-1795, the decades I have laboured in ever since.

*

In the meantime occurred another major development in my life. The Walpole Office was on the third floor of Yale's Sterling Memorial Library. The stack attendant on the third floor, whose job it is to retrieve books for readers, was a young Polish girl, Teresa Marganska, who had emigrated to America with her parents in 1966. When I first saw her she was only 19 (I was 25). We met, dated, I proposed, and we were married on 24 Aug. 1968, just nine days before I began my work as a Walpole editor.

As this point I was still in my agnostic phase. Tess had been raised a devout Polish Roman Catholic, and her parents were both deeply devout. We were married in St. Mary's Irish Catholic Church in New Haven. This choice amounted to a compromise, since my parents and I were still (nominally) Lutheran, and we drew the line at the ceremony being in St. Stanislaus Polish Catholic Church. In any event, Tess had become disillusioned by the authoritarianism of both the Polish Catholic Church and Polish Communist secular society, and we ended up not attending any church for a number of years.

But we had at least what the French philosopher Voltaire called "*la nostalgie de la religion.*" In 1970 we began attending services at the Unitarian Society of New Haven. I was led to Unitarianism by my love of classical music! All through my youth, I had listened to classical music on WQXR, "the radio station of the New York Times." On alternate Sundays WQXR broadcast services from All Souls (Unitarian) Church in New York City. I was attracted by the socially conscious secular humanism of the Unitarians, and persuaded Tess that we should try out the local Unitarian group. (Unitarians call themselves "Church," "Fellowship," or "Society", showing a certain terminological ambiguity about what they are. Historically they are Trinitarians who ultimately rejected the Trinity, then became mainly social activists who leave supernatural matters largely to the individual conscience, at the same time affirming a kind of all-inclusive "spirituality" in the universe.) We found ourselves liking the Unitarians very much (and I still do). They tend to be intelligent, well-educated, and well-meaning. We belonged to the Unitarian Society of New Haven until 1976, when we left for Montreal.

I worked full-time as a Walpole editor from 1968 to 1973. That year I went back to graduate school (Yale this time) to get my Ph.D. In 1974 my volumes of the Walpole Edition were published by the Yale University Press. In the meantime Tess had enrolled as an undergraduate in Southern Connecticut State College, and received her B.S. in Library Science. In 1975 our first child, Nathan, was born.

In 1976 I received my Ph.D. and was offered and accepted a tenure-track position at McGill University in Montreal. I have been there ever since. I went there eventually to become Director of the McGill Burney Project. Frances (Fanny) Burney (1752-1840) was an 18th-century novelist who (like Walpole, whom she knew) left behind a voluminous correspondence. I became editor of her Early Journals and Letters (six volumes, two still to appear), published by Oxford University Press and McGill-Queen's University Press. Thus I continue to do the exact same kind of work I began as a fledgling Walpole editor back in 1968.

*

I have sketched out my career at some length because I want to underscore a continuing moral dimension to my life. Though most of my life I was not particularly "religious," I have always had a very strong moral sense, unquestionably inculcated by my baptism and by the teaching of my mother.

Contrary to the philosophical nihilism and moral relativism that have infected universities at least since the 1960s, I have always believed in the natural law and in moral absolutes. I have therefore always aimed at an absolute integrity and factual accuracy in my scholarly work, and have a horror of the self-aggrandizing and too often dishonest subjectivism that disfigures so much of the work of my colleagues in the academy. (I think particularly of "revisionist" works of biography and history that play fast and loose with the objective record of what was said, done and thought.) I also brought a moralistic slant to my teaching, calling attention to the religious and ethical elements in literary works.

Our daughter Maia was born in Montreal in 1978. Tess was a stay-at-home mom until 1989, raising our two children. That year she entered the McGill Graduate School of Library Science, receiving her master's degree in 1990. She subsequently held a number of part-time jobs until she finally became librarian at the Canadian Pacific Railway, and then at Canadian National Railway. She held the latter job until Dec. 2004, when our lives changed forever.

On 1 Sept. 2004 I took early retirement from teaching at McGill so that I could work full-time on my Burney edition. That month Tess and I took a celebratory cruise to Hawaii. We thought we were sailing off into our "golden years." But God had other plans. On 21 Dec. Tess learned that she had acute leukemia. She was 56. After unsuccessful chemotherapy she had a seemingly successful stem cell implant. But the cancer came back, and she died in the Ottawa General Hospital on 13 Aug. 2005, at 7 in the morning; I was at her side.

A few years after coming to Montreal Tess and I had joined the Unitarian Church of Montreal (formerly Church of the Messiah). We were very active, and I was actually president in 1987-89 (the period when the Church on Sherbrooke St. was burned down by our deeply disturbed organist, with the loss of two firemen's lives). In 2001 Tess and I moved to my present home near Alexandria, Ontario. We started going to the Ottawa Unitarian Church, which was nearer. But we became disillusioned with the heavily socialist slant of most of the congregation. I had also long been disturbed by a strongly anti-Christian element in the Unitarian Church. Many Unitarians are ex-Christians who seem to tolerate virtually anything except Christianity. In 2003, providentially before we learned of Tess's illness, we began attending the United Church in Alexandria. The United Church is of course officially "Christian" (though a recent moderator of the whole church came out as both an agnostic and a doubter of the afterlife!). It is also, of course, the most liberal of the Protestant Christian denominations in Canada. I suppose we chose it because it was just across the dividing line from the Unitarians. Anyway, God was moving both of us slowly but inevitably back to our Christian roots.

Tess died before moving all the way back to her Catholic beginnings, and is buried in the Alexandria United Church cemetery. I very soon erected our headstone there, and in the course of time I will be laid to rest beside her.

*

Her death plunged me into despair. Though I went through the motions, life seemed utterly empty and without meaning. I went to grief counselling, psychologists, psychiatrists. I spoke to my United Church minister. I examined Eastern religions and new age spirituality. I went back to basics, asking myself again those ultimate questions I had largely ignored since my youth: Why am I here? Why is the universe the way it is? Why is there anything at all? Finally my intellectual questions began to resolve themselves into a few basic choices: either the universe is random, or it is meaningful. Either there is a Creator, or there is not. If there is a Creator, the Creator is either impersonal, or personal. I gradually began to see that the scientific scepticism that had burdened me for so many decades was just as much a matter of belief as any of the faiths so scorned by Richard Dawkins and his fellow neo-atheists. I began to see that in fact belief in a Creator was far more reasonable than belief in a random, impersonal universe that had somehow miraculously sprung out of nothing (the Big Bang), ordered itself and then produced personality, self-awareness, conscience, love. I began to believe in a personal, loving God that I had pushed away for so many years but who had pursued me down the decades, "the Hound of Heaven." My belief was aided by a number of powerful signs I have witnessed that tell me that Tess is indeed alive and well (such as a miraculous sunflower that sprung up, only once, next to a little sign in our yard, "Mom's Garden," when all the other sunflowers – 70 or 80 of them – planted by Tess have never come back). In short, I rediscovered the God of Love — the Christian God — the Revealed Holy Trinity of God the Father, God the Son, and God the Holy Spirit.

I continued attending Sunday services at the United Church. I sang in the choir. I attended bible class. As with the Unitarians, I really liked (and still like) the people there. But I never felt really complete there. Memories began to come back to me — Catholic memories. Stamford, the town where I was born and raised, has a very large population of Italian-Americans, almost all of them cradle Catholics. Though I went to public school, I remembered Monsignor Hayes, from St. Mary's Catholic Church, visiting the Catholic students in my elementary school. There is Stamford Catholic High School, and the Sacred Heart Academy. Two of my aunts (by marriage) were Catholic. I remembered being intrigued by — and at some level probably mildly jealous of — the ritual aspects of Catholicism I had seen, in or out of church: the sign of the cross, the incense, the rosary beads, the Hail Mary, the bells, the Latin, etc. I remembered, of course, the deep and unquestioning devotion of my Polish parents-in-law (and their joy at the election of a Polish pope, John Paul II). I felt, at some level, that here was an enormous vibrant family, like no other, that I did not belong to.

I remembered, especially, the kindness of Catholics at times of crisis in my life. Not that non-Catholics, or even non-Christians, had not been kind. But I recalled how Catholic friends of my mother, not especially close friends, had nevertheless offered a mass in her memory when she died, still a nominal Lutheran (as I recall, it was as part of a mass for the conversion of the heathens in Africa!). After Tess died her best friend Marilyn offered a mass for her on what would have been her next birthday, Jan. 24 (a whole range of supernatural signs attended that mass).

\*

But the greatest immediate cause of my eventual conversion was the continuing gentle pressure of my Polish friends Jacek and Barbara Bacz. Barbara and Tess had become friends around 1980, when they were both raising our sets of children. Like Marilyn and her husband Martin, Jacek and Barbara periodically invited me over to visit them after Tess's passing. Jacek has always loved to witness his Catholic faith, and I was eager to wrestle with him over questions of faith and doctrine. Eventually he wore my "anti-Catholic" objections down, until one evening in Jan. 2008, after seven hours of debate (!), he finally said: "Lars, you can wrangle over these matters for the rest of your life, or you can make your move!" Within a week I contacted Fr. Kelvin, the priest at St. Finnan's Cathedral in Alexandria. Fr. Kelvin told me that typically a would-be convert would have to attend RCIA classes from Sept. until Easter. But since I was a professor and good at teaching myself (I had been reading the Catechism and other works), he agreed to meet with me for two hours once a week to monitor my progress towards Rome. The progress was steady, and I was received by the sacrament of confirmation into the Holy Roman Catholic Church at Easter Vigil 2008, celebrated by Bishop Paul-André Durocher. I count this as the day of my true spiritual birth, the flowering of the seed of faith planted at my baptism so many years before.

My friends in the United Church were understanding, in varying degrees, though some were I thought rather too condescending towards my "lapse into popery." Actually, several of them were unwittingly instrumental in hastening my conversion. One lady, not knowing where I was heading, had remarked how once she had visited the Vatican; she airily proclaimed to me that "God was not there." A fellow breathlessly told me about his "discovery" of the Gospel of Thomas (recently republished with a great deal of media hoopla); here was another of those writings suppressed by those rascally Catholics! I'd always been turned off by such blanket condemnations and the ignorance they betray. One of my best friends, Fr. Alvaro Ribeiro, SJ, teaches English literature at Georgetown University. When, out of the blue sky, I informed him of my conversion, he remarked: "You know, Lars, I am not entirely surprised. You have always been an enemy of bull, and a seeker after truth!"

Of course there were problems I had to deal with before my conversion, such as the priestly abuse scandal that had exploded in 2002. But I came to realize that such things (like the Spanish Inquisition, also tossed at me by knee-jerk anti-Catholics) are the result of human sinfulness, and not caused by any of the intrinsic doctrines of the Church. The Catholic world-view in fact holds together beautifully, unlike the multiple and conflicting views of the 20,000 (and counting) Protestant denominations. As for multiplicity, a United Church minister, writing recently in the Ottawa Citizen, has even opined that "there are as many Christianities as there are Christians." In my opinion such radically subjective "theology" is madness, and little different from New Age cafeteria-style spirituality, where the individual in effect cherry-picks those beliefs which are "comfortable." For example: God is all-loving and all-merciful, so there is no hell and we are all saved, no matter what (but where is the God of Justice?). Sola Fides, "once saved, always saved"; therefore it doesn't matter what we do once we believe in Jesus (but what happens, then, to the necessity for good works so often underscored in the Scriptures?).

*

Besides *Sola Fides*, I began to understand the problems with Luther's other reforms, such as the concept of Sola Scriptura. Luther in effect ignored or tried to explain away the fact that the New Testament scriptures arose out of the sacred oral tradition, which therefore in its later written form cannot be ignored for purposes of interpretation. As for the Old Testament, because certain of the "deuterocanonical" books did not agree with his "personal revelation," he simply subtracted them from the canon. When I finally came to the Catholic Church, I discovered all seven of the sacraments instituted by Christ Himself; as a Lutheran I had known only two. As for the Catholic liturgy, suddenly I understood that everything — everything — in it made sense. Those mysterious bells, that incense, the vestments, the genuflections, the Gregorian chants:

these were not superstitious mumbo-jumbo, as I once had been taught to think, but were all beautifully designed to elevate the soul to God. In sum, I had found "the fullness of the faith," the original, true faith, a faith that was practiced daily, and everywhere, and that was indeed "catholic," that is, universal.

Of course, many of these revelations would only come after my conversion. But the clincher in Jacek's debates with me before my conversion, the single argument that motivated me most to make my move, was his defence of the concept of Purgatory, "subtracted" by Luther when he jettisoned the Deuterocanonical Books. It makes such sense that almost no one at death is pure enough to be in the presence of God, and that a spiritual purification is necessary. I thought of Tess, who had left the One True Church and had not yet found her way back into it at her death. I had felt such helplessness, such impotence as a husband as she lay dying. I now know that her awful suffering was her purgatory on earth, and that I now can pray for her departed soul and by my own faithfulness hasten her into the Beatific Vision, wherever she may be now. Such empowerment! Such joy!

In general, perhaps what persuades me most of the truth of the Holy Roman Catholic Church is the magisterial authority of its readings of the Scriptures. As I suggest above, the Protestant emphasis on the individual's interpreting the Scriptures by himself has led to an endless wasteland of error. No one person, however intelligent and learned (like Luther), is capable of understanding by his own lights the Scriptures' incredible riches and subtleties. Only the magisterium of the Church, informed by the early Church Fathers right down to the latest encyclicals of the Pope, can make proper sense of the Divine Word of God. And, most important, a proper reading of the Scriptures affirms the astounding truth of the Real Presence of Christ in the Eucharist, and the profound truth of the apostolic succession, whereby only a Catholic priest or bishop can enable this transubstantiation.

I revise these words the afternoon of Easter Vigil 2009, the first anniversary of my conversion. Nowadays I awake, every day, with a renewed feeling of joy and gratitude to God, along with a renewed desire to work at my conversion (including a resolution to come closer to Mary, a common stumbling block for converts from Protestantism). I recently went on my first Catholic retreat. It was an Opus Dei retreat, and I am immensely attracted by the Work's call to sanctity in one's daily life. Looking back on my own life, I like to think that, by God's grace, I have always aimed at that sanctity, especially in my scholarship and teaching. May I continue to grow in grace and sanctity until that wonderful day when I am reunited with my Tess in the divine light of God's Eternal Love. Amen.

# David Warren

**David Warren has been an editorial-page columnist these last 12 years, in the Ottawa Citizen and other CanWest newspapers; and a contributor to various magazines and now, websites. He founded and edited *The Idler*, of 1984-93, a magazine of "elevated general interest". Other details from what he describes as "a life of sin and error" may be gleaned from the essay itself.**

## Why Catholic?

### I

Among the things I hope to have explained to me, on the Day of Judgement, is why I became a Catholic. This remark is not as frivolous as may first appear. I do not fully understand why I became a Catholic, why I did so when I did, or alternatively, why I did not become a Catholic much earlier in my life. I can explain such things to others better than I can explain them to myself; for what is self-evident to me now, was evidently not self-evident in the past; and a man exists at more than one point of time. This is an important confession to make at the outset, for reasons to which I will return. But to begin, let me say that I become more aware, as I grow older, of the complexity of human motivations, including my own; and that Grace operates upon the whole man, not only in the part of him we see, or he sees.

The question interests me not only for my own case, for I am a born proselytizer. That seems clear enough when I look back – and even from my early childhood, my mother, still living, recalls certain dogmatic tendencies. At age about six, she claims – and I believe her because I remember it – I asked a sceptical question about God. My mother, an atheist then as now, and of the stoical, but merry, Calvinist sort, from Gaelic Cape Breton, had just told me that God made the world. It was her way of avoiding a theological discussion with a six-year-old, who had just asked how the world came to be. She did not realize that I had a supplementary, ambush question up my sleeve. It was: "If God made the world, what was he standing on when he made it?" (To which mama thoughtfully replied: "I don't know.")

No doubt this question had seeped into my consciousness from somewhere in the external environment, for small children do not ask such questions of their own. The notion of infinity soon also seeped in, for within a few years, I had solved the entire mystery of existence to my own satisfaction. The world – the universe – had always been here (or there, if one preferred). It goes infinitely backwards and forwards along the arrow of time; it extends infinitely through space, in all directions. By the age of eleven I could explain, coherently to my peers, that given infinite time, everything must eventually happen. Therefore "everything" can be explained.

Two more years passed by, through which I felt confident in the cosmological powers I could display in any schoolyard. Until, that is, I received my first argumentative setback. For one of my friends was the son of a Dutch Reformed preacher. And in a moment when we were otherwise employed in apportioning newspaper bundles from the paper route we shared, he made a remark that, in one smooth stroke, utterly demolished my theory. He said, and I paraphrase, "What do you mean, 'given infinite time'?" I thought I had taken nothing for granted in my explanation of everything. It turned out I had taken everything for granted.

(Curiously enough, this is exactly what happened in the scientific world, beginning in the late 1920s. The general, long-standing belief that the universe was infinite in all dimensions, fell to pieces in contemplation of the red shift. Though very large, the universe was shown to have a beginning in time, and corresponding limitations in space.)

Jesse was the name of this patient, kindly, and quite intelligent boy. He also generously provided me with a copy of the New Testament, of pocket size. I felt honour-bound to read it. I had recently been presented with an illustrated child's Life of Christ, by a well-meaning adult (my agnostic but dutiful father), and had quietly judged it to be "below my reading level." But I had to admit that the

King James Version was at my reading level, and in places, even somewhat above.

I was an incurable hiker and wanderer as a child. I carried the little book around with me. My friend Jesse seemed to have it all by heart, and could cite New Testament verses by chapter and number like an adding machine. He was not beneath testing me, on my claims to be reading, and from one cause or another I'm sure I pushed through the whole thing. There were several weeks when I hovered on the edge of becoming a very young, born-again Christian. Jesus seemed to be talking to me sometimes. At other times I seemed to be talking to him. He would emerge from the book like the genie out of Aladdin's lamp. I read the Book of Revelation, and had dreams.

In the end I was able to resolve my confusion over religious belief with a three-part strategy: 1. Forget about the book. 2. Avoid Jesse. 3. Gradually develop the "mature" approach to scripture, suggested by an adult confidante; that is, accept "the Bible as literature." Only then could one develop the smug and smooth condescension towards it, which would gain one admission into the chattering classes.

Thus was my first circle completed – the intellectual formation of my childhood. It had begun, curiously enough, in a Catholic school: St. Anthony's, in Lahore, Pakistan. My father had been teaching at the art college in Lahore, and enrolled me in St. Anthony's after my graduation from a certain Mrs. Abassi's kindergarten. He did so because St. Anthony's offered the highest available scholastic standards, not because it was Catholic. I was one of only two befreckled, white-skinned boys in the junior school; the rest were the offspring of the Pakistani elite – very few of them Catholic, either. Or even Muslim, for that matter; I think most of us came from "free-thinking" homes. Only the teachers were Catholic, and as I later learned, some of them only nominally so.

It was an impressively tough school, brutal in some respects; and my childish sense of humour earned me several painful encounters with the school's apparently psychotic principal, a certain Brother Berg. (By sheer coincidence, I met the man's sister in Ireland, much later in life. She told me he had converted to Buddhism, and joined a commune in California.)

I look back on the school fondly, despite the beatings, which were also administered on a free-lance basis by the older boys; and especially upon one adored schoolmistress, a Miss Quinn, who taught me very young to love Shakespeare and Milton, while also exposing me to Jules Verne. (Kipling I found on my own.) Neither she nor anyone else put me under the slightest pressure to become a Catholic; although I do recall being beaten by Brother Berg, first for failing to attend Mass, when he assumed that I was a Catholic; and then for attending Mass, after he discovered that I was a Protestant. (I did try to explain such things to him, but found that such flippancy only made him hit me harder.) I came away from that school with an immense regard for mental rigour, which was indeed being taught. In retrospect, I even long to shelter poor Brother Berg, from himself.

By the end of my childhood (coming and going between exotic foreign places, and a family home in Georgetown, Ontario), I was Miss Quinn's intellectual child, having now adopted the Bible as literature, on the analogy of Shakespeare and Milton (and Jules Verne; Kipling's Kim being the true scripture). Old and New Testaments alike were brimming with poetry, and to be read as fiction, in suspension of disbelief.

As an adolescent, parachuted into the semi-rural catchment of Georgetown District High School, after another season abroad (in Thailand), I was what I called an "evangelical atheist"; verily, the Richard Dawkins of Georgetown High. I went out of my way to proclaim atheism, in classroom and cafeteria alike. And in the latter, I indulged a brutish desire to humiliate innocent young believers, and shake their faith. I turned with special venom upon an otherwise harmless boy, who just happened to be Dutch Reform, and who'd had the audacity to defend himself. I argued with teachers. I talked in the library. I refused to be silent through the Lord's Prayer, and was asked to spend morning exercises in that library (from which I was now banned at other times of day) after an incident in which I had unfurled a prayer rug, used a compass ostentatiously to find the direction of Mecca, and then loudly declaimed the Arabic morning prayer -by way of disrupting the Christians. I thus found myself lumped in – for the duration of morning exercises – with Jehovah's Witnesses, who refused to stand for the national anthem, which of course I sang lustily in their presence.

And then, at age sixteen, I dropped out. I was tired of high school, contemptuous of Canadian educational standards, and eager to see the world on my own.

## II

My adolescent atheism survived to the age of twenty-three, through years when I was travelling in Europe and Asia. I had decided to read philosophy and classics, without guidance. Finding myself in London, in the mid-seventies, with a reader's ticket to the British Museum, a subscription to the London Library, and a very cheap place to live (those were the days of squatters), I resolved on a course of study that consisted of three parts: Aristotle; everything that went into Aristotle; and, everything that came out. By this programme, I was soon becoming at least superficially acquainted with such indubitably Catholic authors as Thomas Aquinas, and such modern Aristotelians as Franz Brentano.

I had no ambition to become a "professional philosopher" – a class of persons I still tend to despise (Socrates never had tenure). Rather, like Socrates, I wished to be philosophical, and to pursue the truth, wherever that might lead.

Footloose in Asia, I had met many travellers West to East, and had formed a particular desire not to become a hippie. My little explorations of Asian societies had left me, moreover, without hope for the future of Buddhism, Hinduism, or Islam, though with some passing respect for what these religions had been. I had cultivated the habits of an "outsider," and was now embarked on what felt like a methodical study of the "Western" past, convinced, by a process of subtraction, that it remained the only viable legacy; and further convinced that I could never become other than a creature of "The West." And the West seemed very impressive to me, coming home to it from Asia.

Once in Europe, I quickly developed something like the modern, sophisticated European attitude towards Christianity, in contrast to the crassness of my own more American, and adolescent atheism. I had by now great respect for "the Church" as a kind of museum and archive of "culture" – to be preserved with all contents as any other ancient subject of aesthetic admiration – ideally by curators, instead of priests. I began to realize, like a sophisticated European atheist, that had there been no Christianity there would also have been no Dante, no Michelangelo, no Bach, and given such omissions, perhaps not even a Wallace Stevens (my favourite poet of the time), nor a Picasso (by whose works I was also then mesmerized). But that was something quite apart from belief, for belief was something we'd "outgrown." Belief was for Americans: it was the crass flip side of their "uncultured" atheism. (And I could think such things without being anti-American in any political sense, for I could see they were still providing the NATO shield that made sophisticated European culture possible.)

And yet there was something that disturbed my dogmatically anti-dogmatic slumbers. This was a growing realization that the overwhelming majority of my intellectual and artistic heroes – even the modern ones – were Christians. This disconcerting realization had started with the glimmering that Thomas Aquinas was no fool, that he was Aristotle's equal or greater in the art of comprehension, acting upon the "science" of his time. But he could be confined safely to the Middle Ages. How was one to excuse the Audens and Eliots, a Czeslaw Milosz, or an Alexander Solzhenitsyn? I took my own cleverness for granted. But how could men otherwise so much greater and wiser be, with respect to religion, less clever than me?

Pound, Eliot, Stevens: they were my literary gods. Pound and Stevens were the greater poets, but Pound was a political idiot, and Stevens, on religion, a very tedious drone. Eliot was the poet with a mind, and I was now reading the Four Quartets, and feeling my own shallowness between every line.

My career as a cultured, sophisticated atheist came to grief, late one afternoon in a library. There were two books on my table at the time. One was Kant's Critique of Aesthetic Judgement, in Meredith's translation, with Meredith's notes, which, as Meredith says in one or another of his prefatory essays, contains an argument that builds gradually and irresistibly, like the speed of a train. I was beginning to glimpse that argument, and with it, a sense that beauty ran parallel with reason, and like reason, could produce results. A long, straining afternoon, wrestling with Immanuel Kant, had set me up for a knock-out.

For the other book on my table was entitled, Speculations. It was by T.E. Hulme, a pioneering English modernist from before the First World War. The library was soon closing, I wanted to get the flavour of the book before going home. I got through a rather vulgar "Critique of Satisfaction," culminating in an intentionally vulgar geometrical demonstration of the idea of "God," that began, spookily, on page 32. On page 33, I read:

> Imagine a man situated at a point in a plane, from which roads radiate in various directions. Let this be the plane of actual existence. We place Perfection where it should not be – on this human plane. As we are painfully aware that nothing actual can be perfect, we imagine the perfection to be not where we are, but some distance along one of the roads. This is the essence of all Romanticism. Most frequently, in literature, at any rate, we imagine an impossible perfection along the road of sex; but anyone can name the other roads for himself. The abolition of some discipline and restriction would enable us, we imagine, to progress along one of these roads. The fundamental error is that of placing Perfection in humanity, thus giving rise to that bastard thing Personality, and all the bunkum that follows from it...

And then, on page 34:

> No 'meaning' can be given to the existing world, such as philosophers are accustomed to give in their last chapters. To each conclusion one asks, 'In what way is that satisfying?' The mind is forced back along every line in the plane, back on the centre. What is the result? To continue the rather comic metaphor, we may say the result is that which follows

the snake eating its own tail, an infinite straight line perpendicular to the plane.

That was in the art library within the Victoria and Albert Museum. It was midwinter – January, 1976 – and I returned the two books to the desk. I walked out of the library, down the grand stairs, through the grand foyer, out onto the dark cold streets of West Kensington. As the winter chill caught up with me (I was always underdressed), I formulated this ridiculous thought: "I am what they call a Deist now. I believe there is a God, immanent and transcendent. My faith in atheism has just been shattered."

## III

Let me explain that I was not terrifically happy about this realization. Rather, I felt almost a broken man. I thought, "Everything I believe is wrong. Everything I know will have to be re-examined, and thought through again from the start. And I will have to tell my friends that I was wrong about everything, that I take it all back. And those stupid Christians are going to laugh at me."

When the tent in which you live blows over, what can you do but pitch it up again? There is nevertheless the question: How? The next morning I got up, in the solid little workman's cottage I then occupied in Vauxhall – thanks to the disastrous housing policies of the socialist Borough of Lambeth, sans utilities but rent-free. I set to work, over the usual buttered scone and tea. I would not have to review all the arguments, I quickly decided, for one pillar from my Temple of Atheism remained standing: there would be no Christ. Christ is for weak people. Christ is myth. Or as I wrote at the time:

> The sort of God I can accept does not become a little man, or show himself to the world as a slab of meat on a stick. I have absolutely no intention of speaking to a priest, or otherwise darkening the doors of churches.

Needless to say, within several weeks, I was re-reading the Gospels. I was trying to dissect them, like a zoologist, to parse them, like a lawyer:

> Who is this Jesus, and how can we distinguish him from his followers, from the evangelists, from the others who appropriate him to their several purposes? Who is this Paul? Is he not the actual founder of Christianity? How can anyone in his right mind believe that Christ was resurrected? That Lazarus, too, rose from the dead? That Christ performed any other miracles? Is this not a childish and primitive account of the divine? How can any sophisticated person buy into all this?

And then, Jesus himself:

> Is he not clearly mad? Are we not reading sanitized accounts of his life and times? He claims to be God's personal messenger, and often more than that. But how can a God whose own existence is beyond the universe, before time, outside space, possibly concern himself with minor historical events in one corner of a very small planet, orbiting a commonplace star, on a spiral arm of one of many million galaxies? It seems to me that Christ makes the existence of man disproportionately large. Far from

being made in God's image, Christ remakes God in man's.

I invested many weeks in this critique; winter turned to spring. The whole of the Bible had become by this time an unfortunate and sometimes loathsome mess, cluttering the beautiful, monolithic simplicity of my idea of God. Give me anything instead, give me the *Tao-te-Ching*, the *Dhammapada*, even the *Koran*. But O, Lord! Please don't give me the *Summa Contra Gentiles*. I was becoming desperate, flailing about.

At least a dozen times, I formed the question in my head, "Jesus, if you exist, don't be coy. You could just show yourself to me." Yet, such was my desperation, that the sarcasm was draining from this question, and my own self-confidence was skulking away. For, depending upon the time of day, I was no longer sure Christ wasn't the answer.

Then one day – Thursday, April 15th, 1976 – I was walking along the Thames south embankment, wrestling with the question once again. By the National Theatre I turned, as I had often done, up the wrought iron steps to the pedestrian gangway that followed the Hungerford Railway Bridge. The trains shunted across this bridge, from Waterloo Station on the south side of the river, to Charing Cross Station on the north side. I had often paused to enjoy them.

Were other persons present? There must have been plenty. Were there any other witnesses? I have no idea. What I do know, is that I had just asked the question, "Jesus, are you there?" without the slightest hint of sarcasm.

Whenupon, immediately, I felt His presence. I cannot adequately describe this, for even though my memory remains vivid, words fail. I felt the presence, not of a light, but of a Person, fully, as if walking beside me; yet not of a man walking, but rather, a source of pure light, pure heat – an irradiation of perfect Love, more real than the world around me, and therefore tending to blot it out. I did not have to ask, "Are you the Christ?" for I knew this already. And I did not have to listen, for I had already heard: "I will cross this bridge with you." And we crossed the bridge, to the north side.

He is gone, I realized, standing above the stairs on that north side. For a moment, I could actually see a Spirit, hanging visibly in the air before me, but with its centre in any direction that I looked, "standing over London." I thought: "This is the Paraclete." I thought, "From my earliest childhood, He has been there, watching over me, in the immanent guise of a guardian angel. This is not something unfamiliar to me, only something I did not understand."

I continued walking, north, but walking only, without a destination, trying to assimilate what had happened. It still did not occur to me, to look for a church. Months passed, before that thought developed into more than a casual notion, and I began to enter various churches, like a thief in the night, sitting always at the back during services, to be first out the door, owing to a mortal fear of coffee klatches. I discovered the SPCK bookshop, in the crypt below St. Marylebone's; I discovered the Catholic Truth Society bookshop; and every other repository of religious books. I read Anglican divines, beginning with the Elizabethans, Richard Hooker and Lancelot Andrewes; and began mastering the Book of Common Prayer. My familiarity with English literature made the English divines more accessible to me than the saints and theologians of the Counter-Reformation, and T.S. Eliot had already given me a taste for their prose, pointing me subconsciously towards Canterbury, not Rome.

## IV

I'd been living like a wandering friar, even before my conversion. I continued in this manner, which I enjoyed. In those days, it seemed, I lived on air. I wandered, almost entirely on foot, all over southern England, and sometimes, after cadging a lift, onto the Continent. This behaviour continued, until I found myself back in Asia with a proper job. I now fully accepted Christ, yet was still wandering nowhere in particular.

At the time just after my conversion, however, I was taking odd jobs, as a stagehand, and the like, whenever I needed cash. One of these jobs was backstage at the Victoria Palace, a squalid old vaudeville theatre, then fallen upon sentimental variety shows, for the de-edification of tourists. I remember with amusement having nothing to do, after a scene change. I was stretched out, reading, on a Freudian settee, that was a stage prop for a comedy routine. Around me, and habitually ignored, were members of the chorus line, in various states of undress, changing costumes between numbers, snorting and rustling, as in a pastel by Degas. They would have assumed I was a homosexual; all the other stagehands were. One of them mischievously crept up behind me, and seized the book out of my hands. It was *Holy Living and Holy Dying*, by Jeremy Taylor – an original folio, though re-bound, from the 17th century, borrowed from the London Library. She read out the full long title to the other girls, whose mocking titters I still recall; as I also recall thinking, "Let me not be distracted."

I am bringing women into this narrative to some purpose, bear with me. Women have been the bane of my existence. My problem is, quite frankly, that I'm attracted to them. My secular-humanist parents provided me with solid instruction, on how to get along, and were themselves the perfect model of faithful married love. I had every intention of following in their footsteps: to find a good woman, have children, &c.

My further problem was poor judgement (I trusted ones I should not, and vice versa), and the sad accident of coming of age at a time when the mores of Western Civilisation had more or less collapsed. I think all of my moral poise had been lost, and to some extent my sanity disturbed, when, at the tender age of nineteen, I found the woman I wished to spend my life with, and gave my heart inconsolably away. To make the story very short, she was not the woman I thought she was. Nor, of course, was this her fault – one must take responsibility for one's own illusions. Still, her infidelity almost destroyed me.

Already stung, to the heart, and then repetitively stung (mere flesh wounds), through the period just after, when I tried to adopt the contemporary mores, as a monstrous retaliation upon the female sex, I had formed a very secular "vow of chastity," and was enjoying the freedom it had won for me. This had all happened prior to my conversion, but now helped me feel holier than I was.

Christ, having appeared, seemed now to have left me to my own devices. My church-shopping left me finally in the Anglican communion, but under the false impression I was a Catholic. I chose Anglicanism because my "now" was in England; because the part of that church to which I was attracted felt very Catholic, in teaching and liturgy. Yet I'd intended at first to become a Roman Catholic, on principle.

Indeed my best friend of those days, Michael, a tall red-haired Scotsman, an unambiguous atheist with a fine analytical mind, had told me to go join the Roman Church. He said, and I think I quote precisely: "Look, if I'd had your religious experience, I wouldn't fuck about. I'd go straight to Rome. Anglicanism is all about the 'middle way.' It's for people who are half way to nowhere."

So partly on the advice of this clear-headed atheist, I did speak, eventually, to a Roman priest. He passed me a copy of the Dutch Catechism, then all the rage among the most self-satisfied of fashionable, liberal Catholics. And as I read that appalling "progressive" document, full of heresies I could already detect, I began to believe that my Calvinist ancestors might have been right. Perhaps the Roman

Church had gone over to the Antichrist. Moreover, I had by then church-shopped a couple of Catholic parishes, and watched with horror their "new, improved" post-Vatican II Mass, which incorporated the worst features of Protestantism. To a person with any appreciation for poetry and art, it was unspeakably vile. It left me actually shuddering with revulsion, after the beautiful smells and bells of High Anglicanism. I simply could not stomach "progressive" English Catholicism, as I then found it presented to me. Yet I had no problem whatever with Transubstantiation, and soon found myself on the "catholic" side of every intra-Anglican feud.

For a quarter century, I remained a believing and reasonably observant Anglican, a Tractarian with a growing anxiety about the later Newman, with whom I could not argue. I watched that church falling apart around me, in England then elsewhere. I endured as an Anglican, with increasing stoicism. I married an Anglican, in an Anglican church, back home in Canada in 1983, and Anglicanism became a background condition of the marriage. As time passed, and woman priests accumulated in the sanctuary, I spoke more and more openly about fleeing to Rome. I had, anyway, by this time, a much larger view of the Catholic Church. But I could not go there without terrible sacrifices – without, very likely, breaking up my family, which now included two beautiful children. It was an extremely unhappy marriage, I had shown catastrophically bad judgement again, but to my "conservative" Anglican view, it was quite indissoluble. Finally the marriage disintegrated anyway, and at the age of almost fifty, I was once again on my own, and as penniless as I had ever been at twenty, thanks to the operation of Ontario Family Law.

And bitter, did I mention bitter? There is no need to go any deeper into my bitterness, whose ultimate causes were of my own making, but whose proximate causes were quite external. I felt the victim of various kinds of treachery; including what felt like treachery in the Anglican church. I felt an anger colder than any I had ever felt before; an anger that prayer did not seem to assuage. I had travelled very far from Hungerford Bridge; and while it was not possible for me to deny Christ, I could feel His absence.

# V

Left with much opportunity to stew, separated from every emotional comfort of hearth and home, and alone now, in middle age, with a loneliness I had never experienced, I reviewed the various disasters of my life. At one point, I fixated anew on my first experience of "post-modern love." I recalled every detail I could, of what had happened in that passionate season, when I had been nineteen: of how my heart had been poisoned. On a holiday, I contrived to go on a crazy fact-checking "pilgrimage" to a house where I had once briefly stayed with this girl, ostensibly for the purpose of comparing my detailed memories with the surviving physical evidence. I wanted to assure myself that the things I remembered had really happened. They had.

This was a drizzling day, in August of the year 2003, and I had no umbrella. It was the first time in thirty years I had looked at that house. Seeing it again, brought back more memories, and chronological connexions fitting into place. For a moment I was truly reliving the past, recalling the very scent of my lost "Eurydice," while incidentally getting soaked to the skin. My mind had become detached from the present.

The truth is that, through thirty years, I had often prayed to forgive and forget, and as often failed to accomplish this. It was unfinished business. There was a very hard place in my heart, and this was precisely where it was located.

Walking away, in continuing drizzle, I came to a Catholic church, named for St. Anthony. I recalled that, by coincidence, this St. Anthony, of Padua, had kept turning up at various hinge moments in my life, generally in the form of bricks and mortar, by the side of a road. I laughed to myself at this, then noticed, in the encroaching darkness, the front doors of this church were open – from the heat of summer – and that blazing light was coming from inside. An evening Mass was being sung, in Brazilian Portuguese. I was dripping wet, I could not make a distracting spectacle of myself by going inside. Instead I made a spectacle on the steps outside, when I suddenly decided it was time to pray, looking in towards the altar.

I invoked not Christ, but Mother Mary, and entreated her to help me. I did not know what to pray, but a thought came. I prayed for this long lost "Eurydice," that wherever she might be – and I had been told she had died some years before – my long-forgotten love for her might fly to her aid. In the very moment this intention was formed, I was freed of my bitterness. The tremendous weight of it was lifted: thirty years of weight.

In the same moment, I apprehended the spirit of Mary, patron of broken hearts. I felt Our Lady sweep over me; I knew she had intervened. A second, indubitably miraculous "experience" had begun its operation on my soul.

# VI

Walking away from that, and pondering, the resolution quickly formed to become a Catholic, and to do so immediately, wasting no more time. I was convinced that Mother Mary herself had instructed me to do so. I walked several miles, but upon returning to my quarters, before even changing my clothes, I made two phone calls. The first was long distance to my own mother, for I thought I better warn her, before she could possibly hear from any other source, that I was crossing the Tiber.

Mama's reaction was swift and droll. She had never understood my Anglicanism, but at least that was "Protestant," and thus within the pale. To become a "Dogan," as they call them in Cape Breton, was to set all one's Calvinist ancestors spinning in their graves; to say nothing of my Methodist ancestors on my father's side, and the Evangelicals in my extended family. No one, but no one, in my

279

family trees, had come anywhere near to Poping, in the whole time since the Reformation.

"But, but, ... they eat Protestant babies!" said mama, upon collecting herself. (She was of course joking.)

"Only at Easter, mama," I replied.

This at least persuaded her that she was speaking to her own son, and not to some dark spirit who had taken possession of his body. My father soon came on the line, with his own characteristic drollness, assuring me that, "I have some medications here for your mother, and I'm sure she will be okay."

My next call was to John Muggeridge, an old and beloved Catholic friend, whom I knew would be delighted. I asked him, practically, "What do I do now?" That wasn't a problem. With military efficiency he went to work. Within minutes, it seemed, he had Father Robinson of the Oratory, onto me like a Doberman. In a flash, I was taking catechetical instruction, at the feet of that true master.

By a happy coincidence, I was also suddenly rendered quite literally homeless, by the machinations of Ontario's Kafkaesque feminist bureaucracy, so that I had suddenly to offload my few remaining possessions – the books I had managed to carry away – and "live like a Marine." All my once formidable bourgeois income was now being seized, by agencies of the State, and I could no longer pay the rent on a very modest apartment.

It was thanks alone to this piece of luck, that John Muggeridge then took me in – he had a spare room the size of a large closet – and for the next year I had the opportunity to live in an entirely Catholic environment, and learn how to cope with rosaries. With the next cash I was able to obtain, I bought a very Catholic Crucifix. This was a blessed year of my life, through all of which, it seemed, everything necessary was arranged for me.

Dear John, a sweet and saintly man, and true friend, who has since died, was of course my sponsor, when I was received into the One Holy Catholic and Apostolic Church, on the 31st December, 2003. By sheer coincidence (I did not choose that date) it was the precise anniversary of the winter day I had left home in Georgetown, decades before, to go out into the world on my own. I had then been sixteen; I had now half-a-century of sin and error under my belt, but some confidence in the path to redemption.

There are many more coincidences I have not recorded here, and many other details of interest to me, that might seem petty and distracting to a reader. A Christian will not be surprised by such things, in which he will instinctively see divine agency, winking at him. Suffice to say I am caught entirely in a Catholic "trap," and can reasonably hope to die a Catholic, for by now the truth of the road before me is confirmed not only by the large facts, but by a supporting myriad of the small.

Yet beyond these there necessarily remain things I do not understand, and likely will not understand, even about my own actions, so long as I must wear this mortal cloak. For I cannot get "behind" Grace. The mystery of free will remains, and the mystery of the causeless action of Love. I acted as I did from explicable causes, but also from inexplicable causes, and perhaps causelessly as well.

## VII

At the outset, I mentioned that it would be easier to explain my Catholic conversion to others than to myself, and hinted at the reason. Reviewing what I have written above, I see a plausible case, for psychological motivations. An atheist could easily argue that my religious development was a response to personal traumas of some kind; he might confidently attribute my religious experiences to the "temporary madness" of hallucination. The Gospels have themselves been often dismissed, and even when partially confirmed historically, the miracles and finally the Resurrection explained as so much "spiritual" fever. Having taken as an axiom that there can be no Christ, and having ruled all evidence to the contrary out of court, it is easy enough to explain all of Christianity away.

Yet I could have told the whole story without mentioning Hungerford Bridge, or the steps of St. Anthony's church. I could instead have presented it, selectively, but consistently, as the history of my own intellectual growth. For prior to the religious experiences that led, first to my conversion to Christianity, and much later, into the Catholic Church, I had in fact devoted much time and effort to studying the issues, and thinking the questions through.

Why, rationally, would one become a Catholic?

A truly open mind – so rare! – will look patiently at all of the evidence, rather than selecting what he wants to see. And having examined the Gospel underpinnings of Catholic claims, he will turn to the history that follows from them.

He will, for instance, consider the whole history of the Catholic Church, distinguishing what is remarkable from what is unremarkable; for incidents of human evil and foolishness within that history are hardly particular to Catholicism. He will ask hard questions about how the Church has survived; how she has recovered again and again from her own terrible mistakes, as well as from external persecutions. More than once, she was near extinction, more than once, recovered against all odds. He will wonder how this Church is teaching, after twenty centuries, more or less (if not precisely) what she was teaching at the end of one. He will notice that such a continuity, institutional as well as doctrinal, is unique in human history. He will be impressed by the extraordinary succession of the saints, found in every generation, as well as by the apostolic succession. He will consider the larger civilization that Catholic Christianity begat; the art and science that made "The West" pre-eminent among the world's recorded civilizations, and in many ways inclusive of all others. He will ask how it comes to be, that Catholics are more widely dispersed over the surface of this planet than members of any other church, religion, or cult – now or ever before in time – and how the Church continues to find new converts in the least likely places.

I had myself to recover from a view of the Catholic Church that began very narrow. In the years after my unpleasant encounter with "post-

Catholic" Catholicism – in London, circa 1976 – I learned more and more about the rest of the history and geography of the Church. The culmination of that intellectual experience was lodging in Casa Nova, the Franciscan hostel in the old city of Jerusalem, towards the end of the 1990s. I heard, with my own ears, the immense diversity of languages spoken along the benches, among the pilgrims taking breakfast in the morning. These were Catholic pilgrims, from every walk of life, who had come to the Holy Land from everywhere on earth. I could not help but contrast that with the Watneys Red parochialism of the Anglican chapel I was attending on Sundays.

Contrast the response itself with the more usual response, to Catholic life and history, inculcated today by our schools and media, which reduce everything to several malicious, Pavlovian lines: "The trial of Galileo!" and, "The Spanish Inquisition!" and, "The bloody Crusades!" And I mean, Pavlovian, for these "facts" will be adduced, quite invariably, by people who know nothing whatever about them, and have not the slightest curiosity to find out.

Long before, in my own more purely intellectual review of Biblical claims, before I became Christian, I found the arguments for Jesus as Christ the more compelling, the more I learned, and the more I thought things through. I had finally to ask myself such questions as: Why, if Christ was not resurrected, would his disciples set about carrying this very specific claim to the ends of the earth? Why would each stick by the story, even to martyrdom? Why, when they had responded to the crucifixion by hiding away?

That was large, but there was also small. Again in the Holy Land, at Capernaum, out of my interest in archaeology, some years ago, I found myself standing over the remains of what was unquestionably the house of Simon Peter, neatly framed by the octagon of a very ancient Byzantine church, and an even older church beneath it. And beneath that, the forensic proofs that this house and its immediate neighbourhood were precisely as described in Matthew and Mark. Here was the toll booth, on the road to Damascus; here was the synagogue at which Christ prayed; here was the alley through which the officer's servant was carried; and here, in the reconstruction of the house, is how he was passed "through an opening in the roof" to Jesus, to be healed. All the evidence of lamp shards, by their style, attested to the date; and much else. The Turin Shroud might be debatable; nothing here was.

This is skimming the surface only, the surface of the surface, and much deeper we could go, while still restricting ourselves to demonstrable facts. Had I never had a religious experience, I would still have the arguments with which to construct Christ and His Church, and to "believe on them." But intellectual conviction is not spiritual conviction: that requires more, not less. An intellectual conviction, that the Christians were probably right, did not convert me; an intellectual conviction that Catholic claims were sound, did not pull me into the Church.

In reading of the conversions of others, whether told at first or second hand, I am often struck by what has been de-emphasized. The writers of such narratives are explaining themselves, after all, as often as not to unbelievers, including the unbeliever who still lurks perilously within every Christian soul. And even after this has been confronted, the ego of a man demands that he should play a starring role in his own conversion. And when that is confronted, human language itself necessarily prefers the tangible to the intangible.

The common feature in all honest accounts of conversion is the operation of Grace. We could not convert ourselves, any more than we could give ourselves birth. In my own case, the operation of Grace was not subtle. That is only, I think, because I presented an extremely hard case; and I often think I could not have been converted by any other means.

But Grace works, overtly or subtly, in every aspect of our lives; and works from everywhere, and from all time. As we progress, in prayer and contemplation, we may become more aware of this operation, and of the omnidimensionality of Love. Ultimately, in the unitive way, we seek the fullest possible integration of this human flesh within the Body of Christ; to overcome the last vestiges of a fleshly rejection.

That is what we seek, in the end, so far as we are we. But from the beginning, the larger truth was that we were sought.